Getting Noticed

Wiley Press books are available at quantity discounts when used to promote products or services. For information, please write to:

Special Sales Dept.
John Wiley & Sons, Inc.
605 Third Avenue
New York, NY 10158

Getting Noticed

A Manager's Success Kit

Dennis J. Kravetz

THE WILEY PRESS
John Wiley & Sons, Inc.
New York • Chichester • Brisbane • Toronto • Singapore

Publisher: Judy V. Wilson
Editor: Elizabeth G. Perry
Managing Editor: Katherine Schowalter
Composition & Make-Up: Ganis & Harris, Inc.

Library of Congress Cataloging in Publication Data

Kravetz, Dennis J.
    Getting noticed.

    Includes index.
    1. Success in business.   I. Title.
HF5386.K835   1985   650.1   84-21980
ISBN 0-471-81507-1

Printed in the United States of America

85   86   10   9   8   7   6   5   4   3   2   1

Contents

Preface

All of us, regardless of our field of endeavor, would like to be successful. Professional success often means getting promotions, salary raises, and prestige. The amount of professional success we attain is one of the yardsticks we use to determine if our lives have been worthwhile and fulfilling.

Behavioral scientists have identified two kinds of people with regard to success (see Bernard Weiner, *Theories of Motivation*). Those in the first group believe success is due to good luck, having friends in high places, or being in the right place at the right time. For these people, success is like a slot machine: maybe they'll get lucky and maybe they won't. These individuals live in the hope that their lucky day will arrive sooner or later, and they will have wealth, power, and fame. Because they simply sit and wait, instead of actively pursuing success, most of these people end up with no significant success at all.

Those in the second group believe they control their lives and can make success happen. They feel that their abilities, skills, planning, determination, and hard work will lead to success. They know they'll encounter obstacles along the way, and they're prepared to surmount them. As you might guess, these people attain greater success and are more satisfied with life than those who rely on luck.

This book is written for individuals who want to attain greater success in business, especially those who want to move into management or advance into higher management. This book explains the style, techniques, and skills that highly successful people use. You'll learn to evaluate your success in a number of areas, and you'll come to understand how you can improve where needed.

Success means different things to each of us. To you it may mean attaining a certain position in your company, reaching a certain standard of living, achieving recognition in your field, being a civic leader, or having others look up to you. Regardless of how you define success, your attainment of it will depend on how vigorously you pursue it. You and you alone can control your own drive toward success. The means for doing so are detailed in this book.

I have spent a number of years as a personnel executive, industrial psychologist, and consultant to business and industry. During that time I have come to know about success not only theoretically but from a practical standpoint as well, by studying individuals from many walks of life who have attained a great deal of success. The highly successful have always fascinated me, and I have made it a point to discover what separates them from less successful people. Over the years I've identified several important skills and personal characteristics that invariably lead to success. These form the topic of each chapter of this book. In addition to these determinants of success, I'll offer specific advice on how to make yourself a successful businessperson.

As you read this book, compare your own behavior to that of the successful people described here. Ask yourself how you can become more like them. Put into practice as many of the suggestions as you can. You will attain great success only if you take action. Knowing how to be successful is not enough; you must act on what you know. This book will help you become a success only if you practice the techniques of successful people until they become part of your natural, day-to-day life-style.

Dennis J. Kravetz

1·
Understanding Yourself

WHAT YOU ARE

Know thyself.
—Socrates

Diving and finding no pearl in the sea, blame not the ocean, the fault is in thee.
—Chinese proverb

Begin your pursuit of success by understanding what you are. You have your own unique strengths, weaknesses, skills, abilities, and interests. Once you have a clear picture of this profile, you can determine those areas where you are most likely to succeed. Highly successful people are very much in tune with themselves. They understand their strengths and weaknesses and have attained a great measure of success by pursuing enterprises in which they can use their strengths. If they have a weakness that hampers their attaining success, they identify it and concentrate on eliminating it. You, too, must cultivate that attitude. Understand yourself, take full advantage of your abilities, and work continuously to eliminate your weaknesses.

Now, start out by evaluating your abilities, your interests, and your personal characteristics.

Skills and Abilities

List on a sheet of paper six or more of the greatest achievements of your life. I'm not talking about a Nobel Prize or Man or Woman of the Year; I mean accomplishments that are important to you as an individual. Write down six things you've accomplished in business, hobbies, school, family life, civic life, or any other area. Here's a sample list:

- Received a promotion to sales manager
- Published an article on employee motivation in a magazine
- Was the leading salesperson in the central division for two years
- Elected president of condominium association
- Built own home by coordinating the work of various contractors
- Served as treasurer for church board

Now, list the specific skills and abilities you used to accomplish each achievement. Was it your planning and organizing? Creativity? Physical abilities? Math or science skills? Ability to manage people? Attention to detail? The following categories will help you determine which skills were most important for you:

- Manual dexterity
- Athletic ability
- Clerical skills
- Numerical skills
- Leadership ability
- Planning and organizing skills
- Skill in oral and written communications
- Instructional ability
- Ability to assist people
- Artistic and musical talent
- Research skills
- Scientific knowledge

Revise the order of the skills and abilities you used for each achievement, listing the most important ones first. Next, examine these lists of skills and abilities to see what patterns have emerged. Which skills and abilities did you use most often in attaining your achievements? Does your present job take advantage of these skills and abilities? Does it allow you to do what you do best? Are there other positions in your company that would allow you to make use of your unique skills and abilities?

Suppose your analysis shows that you have entrepreneurial skills you could use to establish new businesses. However, as an accounting manager, your job offers you no opportunity to use these skills. Start listing other jobs at your firm that might better match your abilities. Is there, for example, a department that plans and sets up subsidiary offices? Can you plan an eventual move to that department so as to better use your particular talents? Your purpose here is to match your skills and abilities with a career area so you can attain a great deal of success. If your current job provides these opportunities, you need not worry. But if the match is inappropriate, think about other jobs that would make better use of what you have to offer.

Highly successful people have found the career to which they are ideally suited. Often their jobs have been unique or nontraditional occupations, so if your ideal job does not now exist, think about the possibility of creating it. Perhaps you'll have to create the job from scratch, but think first about combining existing jobs into a new position that will suit you. Attaining extreme success depends partly on finding a particular job that matches your interests and abilities.

If you are not in the right job, then your first goal is clear: to obtain a more suitable position. Don't change companies if you like the one you're with now (more about that in Chapter 10). Just look for—or create—a position that suits you perfectly.

Career Interests

You need interest as well as ability to succeed in any given field. If you have the ability to play football, but no interest in the game, you will probably not succeed as a football player. Similarly, if you have great interest in football, but no ability, success will not likely result. Fortunately for most people, ability and interests go together. As you become interested in certain activities, you spend more time developing skills in those areas. If you encounter early success, you become more interested, develop still more skills, and so on in an endless cycle.

Take a long, hard look at the things you're really interested in. What do you spend your time reading, talking, and thinking about? If your answer to that question is "Nothing" or "Everything," you're going to need some help in identifying your interests. Here are some sources of assistance:

- Commercially available tests such as John Holland's *The Self-Directed Search*, or career guidance books that may be available in a nearby library
- A professional counselor who specializes in job guidance
- A job encyclopedia such as the U.S. Department of Labor's *Dictionary of Occupational Titles*
- People who work in various fields and who are willing to explain their jobs to you

Learn as much as you can about various careers from as many sources as possible. Ask yourself, "Would I be interested in this type of career? Would the work be fascinating?" Be certain your interest is based on a full understanding of the career area and is not just a passing fancy. Once you have obtained all the information you need, list your career preferences in order, from most to least preferred. Compare this list with the list you made earlier of occupations that best match your skills and abilities.

Do the careers you are most interested in match well with those that take advantage of your best abilities? Concentrate your efforts on finding a career in which you can take advantage of your skills and interests. Take action to change things. Get into an area where you have a chance to be a superstar.

Personality Traits
You need to understand your own personality, those unique traits that make you different from other people. A self-assessment of your personality traits will show if you have the right

temperament for a given career area. As a simple example, if you are introverted, you will probably not want to pursue a career in sales, no matter how interested you may be in that field. An introverted person will be uneasy with the constant contact with people required in sales. Another career might suit you better.

One simple way to discover what your personality is like is to ask others. Seek out someone—spouse, friend, co-worker— whose opinion you trust and ask that person to describe you. Encourage the person to describe with candor your personality, attitudes, and temperament.

Be prepared for some surprises. When they happen, ask for specific examples. What exactly did you do or say to cause this person to describe you as "overconfident" or "excessively talkative"? Do not be hurt or insulted by anything you hear, and do not defend your behavior or make excuses. That would be unproductive. Your purpose right now is to see yourself as others see you. Later on, you can take action to change those characteristics that you don't like.

Compile a list of the words that the person used to describe you. Does the list please you? Is this the way you want to be seen? Are any of your personality traits preventing you from attaining success? If so, what can you do to change your behavior?

In summary, the first step toward managing your own success is to understand yourself—your abilities, interests, and personal traits. If you are not appropriately matched in your current career, you will find it exceedingly difficult to attain great success. You must be appropriately matched in a career that takes advantage of your unique strengths. Give careful thought to understanding yourself and undertake any changes that will improve your chance at success.

NOBODY'S PERFECT

> *If you feel you have no faults —that*
> *makes another one.*

> *Analyzing what you haven't got as well as what you*
> *have is a necessary ingredient of a career.*
> —Grace Moore

If you have thoroughly assessed your abilities, interests, and personal traits, you've probably turned up some faults. You may lack certain skills, for example, and you may have a few undesirable personality traits. Now is the time to do something about those weaknesses. Take them seriously; don't dismiss them as unimportant. They may be —in fact, they almost certainly are— harming your chances of becoming successful, so you must root them out and replace them with skills and characteristics that will get you ahead.

Most highly successful people firmly believe they are competent; they have strong self-confidence, but they are always willing to look at themselves honestly and to identify the areas in which they need to improve. Then they work hard at changing so that they continually get better and better. Those who believe they have no faults stand still.

Extremely successful people have their own unique composite of strengths and weaknesses just like everyone else. They lack certain skills and abilities, and they know it. But unless those weaknesses hamper their success, they know there is no need to be concerned about them. If a successful business executive cannot kick a football forty yards, so what? Similarly, if a professional football player cannot develop long-range strategic plans, so what? The key is to be good at what you need to be good at. Maintain a strong belief in yourself and your ability to succeed, but be willing to identify and improve any weaknesses that could hamper your success.

Let's take a look at a customer service engineer at a computer company—I. M. Perfect—who refuses to admit his weaknesses. He is talking to his boss—U. R. Notperfect.

U. R. Notperfect: I. M., thanks for stopping by. I wanted to talk with you about complaints I've been getting from some of our customers. They say you've been taking a long time to return their calls. The customers are concerned, because they need to correct their computer problems as soon as possible. Why does it take you so long to get back to them?

I. M. Perfect: Some of our customers bug me all the time with minor problems. When I'm busy working on someone else's problems or completing my paperwork, I don't want to be bothered with phone calls. I get back to them soon enough. There's no problem at all in my mind.

U. R.: But I'm sure you know that when someone's computer is not operating, that person is losing money. The customers don't expect you to rush right over, but at least talk to them on the phone. You might be able to tell them how to solve the problem themselves.

I. M.: I just don't have time for that. I'm one of your best engineers. If you don't like the way I do my job, then you can just get someone else.

U. R.: You are a good employee, and you're an expert at repairing computers. But you have to recognize that returning phone calls and servicing our customers is also part of your job. I want you to work at doing this better.

I. M.: I don't want to be bothered with phone calls when I'm busy. Why not have the secretaries return the calls?

U. R.: The secretaries can't diagnose what's wrong with a customer's computer. The customer needs to talk with you.

I. M.: I don't want to be told I'm not doing a good job! Try and get somebody else to do it better if you think you can!

From this short scene, you can see that I. M. Perfect was unwilling to acknowledge his own shortcoming. I. M. will never grow or get ahead because of his attitude. He might be technically knowledgeable, but will never really be successful unless he admits his weaknesses and sets out to eliminate them.

Consider an alternative response to the same situation. The employee in this scene is Will N. Tolisten.

U. R. Notperfect: Will, thanks for stopping by. I wanted to talk with you about complaints I've been getting from some of our customers. They say that you've been taking a long time to return their calls. The customers are concerned, because they need to correct their computer problems as soon as possible. Why does it take you so long to get back to them?

Will N. Tolisten: It's really a problem with priorities. I have so many things to do all at once that sometimes the calls just slide by. But I didn't realize our customers were upset.

U. R.: They don't expect you to drop everything and pay them a visit, but you could at least advise them over the phone or set up a time to go out and look things over.

Will: I realize now that I've got a problem.

U. R.: What can you do to improve the situation?

Will: I'll make returning phone calls a top priority. That should help improve things.

U. R.: I agree. Will, you have done a fine job for us and you are one of our best employees. I'm confident that you'll return phone calls more promptly. Thanks for your cooperation.

This engineer showed a willingness to look at himself honestly and to acknowledge that he could do better. As a result, he will grow, develop, and become a better performer on the job. This will undoubtedly lead to further success. Will has exhibited one characteristic associated with success: he still remains confident of his ability, but he'll work hard to become even better.

In summary, you can do several things to help identify and correct your weaknesses:

- *Acknowledge your weaknesses.* When someone points out one of your weaknesses, accept that person's judgment and assume that you are doing something wrong.
- *Do not defend yourself.* If you make excuses for yourself, you will never correct your weaknesses and, therefore, never attain great success.
- *Concentrate on eliminating only those weaknesses that relate to your career.* Your other shortcomings—your inability to kick a football, for example—can wait, forever if necessary, for your attention.
- *Remain self-confident.* The fact that you have recognized certain weaknesses doesn't mean you are doomed to fail-

ure. Always keep in mind that you have more strengths than weaknesses and that you are headed straight for success.

To attain success you must capitalize on your strengths. The highly successful know this and have found career areas that effectively use their strengths. However, they also know they must eliminate their weaknesses. The highly successful already have a great deal of strength, and they gain more through additional development. Through all of this their self-confidence remains strong. That is a healthy, positive attitude. Feel the same way about yourself.

IT'S YOUR OPINION THAT COUNTS

Don't worry about what people think of you. They aren't thinking of you, but of themselves.

It matters not what you are thought to be, but what you are.
—Latin proverb

While others can help you better understand yourself, it is your opinion of yourself that matters most. Belief in yourself is critical in attaining success. Highly successful individuals are self-confident and believe in their ability to accomplish great things. Only if you firmly believe in yourself will your subconscious self drive you on to greater and greater achievements. And as you achieve more, you will believe in yourself more strongly. That will lead to still greater achievements, and so on in a never-ending cycle. But you have to start someplace or this cycle will never get going. The time to start believing in yourself is now.

You can use a number of techniques to raise your opinion of yourself. These techniques will not only help you be more successful but will also help you identify other successful people, which will be of use when you hire a staff. Here are some important opinion-strengthening techniques you can use:

Recognize Your Importance

Convince yourself that you are a gifted person who is capable of succeeding. Belief in your ability to succeed must be a sincere, deep down, feeling. Convince your subconscious self of that belief as well as the people around you. Review those things you do well and recognize that your ability profile is just as good as anyone else's, probably better than most people's. Self-confidence is crucial to attaining success.

Talk Like a Successful Person

It is easy to separate successful people from those less successful by the way they talk. Less successful people say things like this:

- "I'm not very good at that."
- "Gee, I never seem to do anything right."
- "I don't think we'll be able to do it."
- "The reasons I couldn't get it done are . . ."
- "I tried hard, but . . ."
- "We'll never get this done on time."

When you hear people talk like that, you know they are not successful. Their conversation suggests they lack confidence in themselves and in their ability to succeed. Contrast that with the way highly successful people talk:

- "I'm confident we can get the job done."
- "I'm very pleased with the way it turned out."
- "We did a good job at that."
- "If we all work a little harder, we can get it done."
- "I know everything will turn out all right."
- "I'm happy with what I've accomplished so far."

These comments show confidence. They indicate a strong ego and trust in others. Practice speaking confidently. It will contribute to your success.

Have a High Opinion of Others

The people who work for you must have a high opinion of themselves. You, as their boss, can strengthen or weaken your employees' opinions of themselves. If you say, "I don't think you can do it," your employees will believe you, and they probably will not do it. However, if you express confidence in them—"I know you can get the job done"—the employees will be much more likely to succeed.

If an employee cannot do the job, and therefore, does not earn your high opinion, then you need to confront that person and correct the problem. But be certain that you don't induce poor performance by failing to express confidence in your staff. Getting others to believe in themselves will enable them to accomplish more and help you reach your goals as well. Express your faith in others whenever you can.

Praise Yourself Silently

Overt expressions of your high opinion of yourself and others are vital, but you should express your feelings inwardly as well. Enjoy the praise that others give you, and then silently reinforce it. Say to yourself, "I did a terrific job on that marketing report. The boss was pleased, and my staff was proud of me. I'm getting better and better all the time."

By doing this, you will maintain a good self-image. You will then behave in a manner consistent with this subconscious opinion of yourself. You will become what you have privately convinced your inner self to become.

IMPROVEMENT, THE KEY

It is right to be contented with what we have, never with what we are.
—Douglas Mackintosh

Our business in life is not to get ahead of others, but to get ahead of ourselves —to break our own records, to outstrip our yesterday by our today, to do our work with more force than ever before.
—Stewart B. Johnson

Develop an improvement plan for every weakness you identified in your self-assessment. This plan will include all the steps you need to take to improve each of your weaknesses. Incorporate into the plan a deadline for each improvement. Give yourself two months, say, to correct one fault and one year to correct a major weakness. Measure your progress by comparing your original behavior to the behavior you are striving to attain, not against the behavior of others. For example, you might want to increase your skill and confidence as a public speaker. If so, then compare each of your own public talks to your previous talks. Don't compare yourself to a professional lecturer. That will simply depress and discourage you. Keep in mind that it took that professional many, many years to develop such great skill.

Experts are made, not born. They have to develop their skill in a gradual, step-by-step fashion. They keep improving and reaching for an ideal goal, making each accomplishment greater than the one that preceded it. The expert in a given area continually aspires to greater and greater things with no end in sight. The executive who earns a million dollars a year aspires to earn two million. The running back who rushes a thousand yards a year wants to rush two thousand yards. That attitude is one reason such people are so successful. They are never content with their current status and always aspire to do more.

Consider now the content of your improvement plan. Identify the specific targets for improvement. You might start with this list:

- Become skilled at corporate planning.
- Learn to access computer-based information.
- Increase skill at developing and conducting performance appraisals.
- Improve the quality of written memos and reports.

When you have listed the things you need to improve, write out your step-by-step plan, including the deadlines for making improvements. Two examples follow:

Goal
Become skilled at corporate planning.

Steps	Deadline
1. Take two courses in planning at local university.	January 1
2. Read one book on the subject.	March 1
3. Read a corporate planning journal.	Once a month
4. Join a corporate planning association.	June 1
5. Attend a workshop on corporate planning skills.	February 15
6. Visit with two local experts in the area.	December 31

Goal
Learn to access computer-based information.

Steps	Deadline
1. Take the company-sponsored course on data processing fundamentals.	August 1
2. Read computer manual thoroughly.	September 15
3. Practice exercises contained in computer manual.	October 15
4. Write two sample programs.	November 15

Show your improvement plans to your boss to make him or her aware of your goals. Your boss might be able to suggest other ways in which you can reach your goals. In addition, you may need management support to participate in a company tuition reimbursement program or in a professional association. Keeping your boss informed of your activities will help ensure the success of your improvement program.

Take advantage of all available resources. Those resources include, but are not limited to:

- College and university courses
- Workshops and seminars
- Professional associations
- Contacts within your company
- Contacts at other companies
- Individual study (books, journals, audio cassettes)

Use a log or a progress sheet to record how you are doing. After each action step, record statements like "complete" or "in progress." This will let you see at a glance exactly how far you've gone in your improvement plan.

Record actual work results wherever possible. For example, if your goal is to reduce the number of errors in your department, keep a weekly record of actual errors. Put this information on a chart or table, so that you and your staff can see your progress.

Some improvement goals are highly complex and may take a number of years to accomplish. But Michelangelo did not learn to paint in a weekend, and Henry Ford did not establish his automobile empire overnight. As long as you keep making progress toward your goal, you are on your way to success. You can continually set more difficult improvement plans to ensure that you never quite get to the end. And you should enjoy considerable success along the way.

WHEN THE GOING GETS TOUGH

> *Life is a series of experiences, each one of which*
> *makes us bigger, even though sometimes it is hard to realize this.*
> *For the world was built to develop character, and we must learn that*
> *the setbacks and griefs which we endure help us in marching onward.*
> — Henry Ford

Crises provide an excellent opportunity to better understand yourself. Under such circumstances the real you is visible more clearly than in normal conditions. The controlled, rational behavior you show under normal circumstances may give way under stress. In a crisis, there is little time to labor over your decisions, conflicting demands are made on you, and stress results. How effectively you can manage the crisis and stress is another factor that will determine how successful you are going to be.

Everyone faces a number of crises. Take, for example, H. Ross Perot, the founder of Electronic Data Systems Corporation. Perot lost a billion dollars when his EDS stock plunged dramatically in 1969. He and the company recovered; his stock today is again worth approximately a billion dollars.

Crises permit you to demonstrate your skills. For example, if a supervisor in a steel mill can turn out a high-quality product even when some equipment is malfunctioning or when the work crew is reduced, this shows unusual ability that wouldn't be seen under normal conditions. An average performer might not be able to do as good a job under those conditions. A crisis gives you an opportunity to show what you are made of. Take advantage of adverse situations when they occur.

Managers will look for your ability to handle crises when they consider you for promotion. Don't become known as a person who can't handle stress and pressure.

In the past have you managed stressful events effectively? Did you perform as well as under normal conditions? Better? Did you emerge as a leader during the crisis? If you tend to go to pieces during a crisis, develop an improvement plan. You can improve in this area by learning relaxation techniques, becoming physically fit, talking out problems with others, and building more confidence in yourself.

Successful people see crises as challenges that allow them to demonstrate their mettle. They do not become unraveled. Instead of saying, "What am I going to do?" they say, "I'll see to it that everything turns out all right." Their confidence goes a long way in inspiring others to work with them in overcoming crises. That's the kind of confidence you're aiming at.

2.

The Plan

GOAL SETTING

> *Parties who want milk should not seat themselves on*
> *a stool in the middle of a field in hope that the cow will*
> *back up to them.*
> —Elbert Hubbard

> *A life that hasn't a definite plan is likely to*
> *become driftwood.*
> —David Sarnoff

If you want to be a success, you must have a plan. You need to
know what you want to accomplish, how you are going to accomplish it, and when. Having goals will not guarantee your
success, but it certainly enhances your chances of attaining
success.

Most people spend more time planning their vacations than
they spend planning their lives. If you ask your friends how they
plan to spend their vacation, they'll tell you precisely when they
are going to leave, when they will arrive, what they plan to do,
and where they will go. But if you ask the same friends what
plans they have for their careers or what life goals they've set,

they're likely to answer in a general way, "I want to be happy," or "I want to be rich."

Why don't people have life and career plans? Probably because they were never taught about such planning in school or any place else. Did you ever take a career or life planning course in high school or college? Most of us have not had any exposure to life and career planning, yet this is essential for attaining and monitoring success.

Success results from accomplishing a long series of specific goals, one right after the other. You can set whatever goals you choose, make them as difficult or as easy as you want, and use whatever timetable suits you best. Then you can evaluate your progress as the years go by and judge for yourself whether or not you have attained success. But the starting point is to map out exactly what goals you want to attain.

The following steps should be used to develop effective goals:

1. Develop goal categories. These categories might include career, financial, civic, family, and personal goals. Some goals might fall into more than one category, but this presents no problem. For example, obtaining an M.B.A. degree might fulfill a personal need and at the same time help you attain a career goal. If you can fulfill more than one need by attaining a goal, so much the better.

2. In each category, list the specific goals you wish to attain. Each goal statement should tell what you want to accomplish, when it is to be accomplished, and how you will measure the accomplishment. Begin each goal statement with an action verb. Here are some useful verbs: start, complete, attain, increase, buy, develop, build. Make your goals specific and realistic.

3. List the action steps you are going to take to accomplish each goal. Establish a completion date for each step.

4. Buy a daily calendar and mark on it the dates for completing each step and goal.

5. Check off each step as you attain it.

6. Reward yourself appropriately for achieving each step.

Now look at some examples of goals placed in appropriate categories:

Career goals

1. Complete M.B.A. degree by June 30, 19—.
2. Become department manager by December 31, 19—.
3. Become division director by December 31, 19—.
4. Start part-time consulting business during 19—.

Financial goals

1. Increase overall earnings by 20 percent during the next year.
2. Buy larger home in the $200,000 price range within the next four years.
3. Earn $100,000 a year by 19—.

Personal goals

1. Run four miles a day by December 31, 19—.
2. Lose fifteen pounds during the next year.
3. Learn to control temper by June 30, 19—.

Civic goals

1. Obtain a seat on the Board of Education within three years.
2. Receive appointment to Art Institute Advisory Board within two years.

Note that these goal statements specify what is to be done and when. The goals are measurable, specific, and realistic.

Next look at specific steps for accomplishing two of these sample goals.

Goal: Complete M.B.A. degree by June 30, 19—.

Activity	**Completion Date**
1. Apply for admission to College X.	March 15, 19—
2. Complete two courses during fall semester.	January 15, 19—
3. Complete two courses during spring semester.	June 30, 19—

Goal: Increase overall earnings by 20 percent during the next year.

Activity	Completion Date
1. Start part-time consulting firm.	February 1
2. Print brochures and other descriptive information.	February 15
3. Distribute flyers to 500 firms and contact 100 other firms by phone.	March 31
4. Obtain contracts worth $15,000 with one or more firms.	June 30
5. Complete consulting work with initial clients.	December 31

Develop both specific annual goals and more general goals targeted three to five years down the road. You can modify the longer-range plans annually if necessary.

Most highly successful people have many goals to accomplish, and most have used a goal-setting process throughout their lives. Goal setting should be a part of your life, too. By using a goal-setting procedure, you will be a step ahead of many others on the road to success.

THE VALUE OF GOALS

We often are so busy putting out fires that we find it difficult to do the planning that would prevent those fires from occurring in the first place.
—Gustav Metzman

It is not enough to be busy; so are the ants. The question is: what are we so busy about?
—Henry David Thoreau

Setting goals helps you focus on important activities and eliminate the irrelevant ones. Without goals, it's easy to get caught up in busywork that does not help you become a success. There is a big difference between being busy and accomplishing important goals. Knowing the difference often separates winners from losers.

Consider the extremely busy executive who was developing performance objectives with the help of a consultant. At the end of the meeting the consultant asked him, "What objectives did you accomplish today?"

He replied, "I went to two meetings, I wrote a memo, and processed the mail in my in-basket."

"No," the consultant persisted, "I asked what *objectives* you accomplished today."

To this the executive replied, "I just told you. I went to two meetings, I wrote a memo . . ."

The consultant handed him the list of objectives they had just drawn up and said, "Which of these objectives did you accomplish by doing all those things today?"

After a few seconds the executive said, "I get your message. I could have used my time more profitably by concentrating on these objectives instead of less important matters."

Like that executive, you can let busywork distract you from the important goals you want to accomplish. Ask yourself whether the activities you do are related to your goals. If your goal is to start your own business or earn an extra $30,000 a year by turning a hobby into a part-time job, then watching television or practicing your putting is not likely to help you accomplish these goals. If you never attain your goals, you can blame only yourself. Enjoy some free time, of course, but engage every day in purposeful actions directed toward reaching your goals.

You can take several actions to keep yourself on the track:

Set Aside Time to Work toward Goals

Schedule a specific time each day to work on a goal, just as you would schedule a meeting or business appointment. Set aside fifteen minutes to an hour or more, and make yourself inaccessible during that period. Have phone calls held and close your office door so you can concentrate fully on the goal in front of you. This will ensure that you spend time each day on important goal-related activity.

Set Up a Reminder System

After you break each goal down into specific steps, each with a completion date, write these dates on separate pieces of paper and file them in chronological order. Each morning you can look in this reminder file and note the approaching deadlines. You can then set aside an appropriate period to work on each activity.

Establish Priorities

Put your most important goals high on your priority list. Give busywork a low priority and work on it only when time permits.

Delegate Responsibilities

Delegate as much of your work as possible to your staff. This will give you additional time to work on your high-priority goals.

Goals are clearly valuable in attaining success. They help you weed out and concentrate on important activity, and they keep you moving in the right direction. In business and industry, those who attain tough long-term goals stand out for having achieved something out of the ordinary. Setting goals and monitoring your progress toward them should become a habit.

LONG-RANGE PLANS

Gutzon Borglum, the sculptor who created the Mount Rushmore memorial, was once asked if he considered his work perfect. "Not today," he replied. "The nose of Washington is an inch too long. It's better that way though. It will erode to be exactly right in ten thousand years."

Recognize right now that it may take you years to reach your ultimate goal. To get where you want to go, you need long-range plans. These plans will give direction to all the day-to-day activities you must perform to achieve the higher goals. Without such long-range plans, you'll be tempted to go for short-term gains at the expense of greater but more distant achievements.

A top executive, for example, may be tempted to trade off long-range gains for short-term profits to appease stockholders and to make himself or herself look good at the moment. This executive might sell company assets or postpone needed improvements in an attempt to make bottom-line profits look good in one year. But people who operate this way will eventually find themselves "available for a new assignment." Immediate short-term gains do not necessarily add up to long-term success. The long-range plan is the better guiding principle in almost all instances.

Another example of the dangers of choosing short-term gains instead of long-range goals is the employee who changes jobs to gain a salary increase. While the increased pay is attractive enough, the person may forfeit vacation, pension, and other benefits that have accumulated over the years at the former place of employment. When the value of these benefits is taken into consideration, the result may be no gain at all, or even a loss in the total compensation package. Clearly, long-range career goals would have been a better way of guiding one's career.

Since attaining a high degree of success takes a long time, your ability to work on long-range plans will help to determine how much success you attain. If you continually look for that short-term, immediate gain, then success may be elusive. Review the decisions you make to ensure you are not reaching for short-term gains to the detriment of long-term success. Always maintain your long-term perspective.

THE TOUGHER THE BETTER

*The greater the difficulty, the more glory in
surmounting it. Skillful pilots gain their reputation from
storms and tempests.*
—Epicurus

*Aim at the Sun, and you may not reach it, but your
arrow will fly higher than if aimed at an object on a
level with yourself.*
—J. Hawes

Not failure, but low aim, is a crime.
—Ernest Holmes

Most successful people set difficult, but achievable, goals for
themselves. Reaching these difficult goals may take time, effort,
and skill, and may sometimes result in frustration. Some people simply cave in under this frustration. They say, "What's the
use of trying? I'll never make it." But successful people frequently see frustration as a challenge. They say, "This is really
tough, but I know I can do it." That attitude is more likely to
lead to success. Set your goals reasonably high, and keep your
belief in your ability to reach them—recognizing full well that
you'll risk some disappointments along the way.

Here are three ways in which you can enhance your goal-
setting procedure:

1. Set your ultimate goals at least three years into the future.
   This gives you time to adapt your plans to compensate for
   minor setbacks and also lets you experience numerous
   short-range successes that build toward that difficult goal.
   As an example, you may set the following difficult goal:
   Earn over $100,000 a year as the owner of my own busi-
   ness in five years. To achieve a goal like this in less than
   five years would be too difficult, assuming you are not already close to accomplishing it. That failure could be very
   frustrating and cause you to give up on the entire goal-

setting process. If you give yourself a few years to attain the goal, you can progress toward it one step at a time, making changes as you go along and seeing your progress toward that goal.

2. Break down your ultimate goal into smaller goals—sub-goals. For example, you could break down the above goal into two sub-goals: (a) get an M.B.A. in three years; and (b) turn a part-time job (completing income tax returns) into a business enterprise in two years. Now break down the M.B.A. goal still further: (a) apply for admission to College X by January 1; and (b) complete two courses in the M.B.A. program by July 1. That done, divide the income tax goal into three sub-goals: (a) advertise the business in the newspapers and in brochures by September 30; (b) double the volume of the business by March 15; and (c) hire a part-time assistant by September 30. Of course, there is no end to how far your sub-goals can be broken down. The important point is to set achievable short-range goals that let you see your progress and build toward more difficult accomplishments. As you reach each sub-goal, you will build the confidence you need to go after that difficult ultimate goal.

3. Reward yourself each time you reach a sub-goal. For example, when you complete your first two M.B.A. courses successfully, take yourself out to dinner at an elegant restaurant, buy yourself a new outfit, or treat yourself to a new record or book. Withhold rewards, of course, if you fail to achieve the goal.

Always link the reward with your success. Say to yourself, "I am buying this new book because I doubled the volume of my tax business before March 15." This will help you set up a long-term behavior pattern for success. You are, in effect, conditioning yourself to behave in a certain way.

You should also take a careful look at the goals that others set for you. Are they too low? Could you do more than your boss is asking you to accomplish? Can you increase the difficulty of your assignments so that they will lead to more significant accomplishments?

Don't set your goals so high as to ensure failure, of course, but do raise them just enough to make your work more challenging, to increase your own achievement, and to make your employers aware of your abilities.

Suppose that your boss has given you two weeks to complete a project report on the benefits your company might offer to its employees. Here's how you can raise that goal: add significantly to the project's scope by comparing the costs of all the benefit options and then recommending those benefits that offer the best value to the company—and have the report done within two weeks. You have set and achieved a higher goal for yourself, and you have shown your employers that you are an exceptional performer.

Raising your goals in this way may increase your work load in the short run, but it will eventually set you apart as a high achiever, a person who consistently does more than is required. This kind of performance will get you noticed—and rewarded.

Another technique for increasing your performance is to take on more goals than your peers. If everyone else has six goals for the year, then you need seven. Do others try to sell a hundred widgets during the year? Okay, then you will sell a hundred widgets *and* set up a system for developing new accounts and tracking renewable accounts. This will set you apart from your peers as an exceptional performer who can succeed at a high level.

Another way to raise your goals is to take on projects no one else has bothered with. If you see a job that needs to be done, don't wait for your boss to assign it to you; take the initiative and do it yourself. If you do not have the resources to complete the project, go to your boss with a specific suggestion as to how you could get the job done: "With the help of one part-time computer programmer, I could reschedule the work on that construction project so as to save three thousand dollars a month in overtime pay, and I could do it by the end of next week." If you get the programmer and complete the rescheduling, you'll get credit for saving the overtime pay. This technique will increase your work load for a few days, but that's exactly what you want right now—a chance to show that you can achieve more goals, and higher goals, than your peers can.

Get yourself into a cycle that goes like this: set goals, attain goals, reward yourself, set more difficult goals, attain those goals, reward yourself, and so on, endlessly. Don't get discouraged if you're not rewarded by your superiors each time you attain a goal. If you show resentment when you fail to receive a promotion or a raise, you'll look like a loser. Keep in mind that it's impossible for the boss to reward you for each achievement. Promotions and salary increases can't be distributed weekly. Keep rewarding yourself, and learn to enjoy the feeling of accomplishment that comes with achievement.

One final means of helping yourself attain your goals is to visualize yourself in the future. Imagine yourself attaining your ultimate goal and enjoying it. Many successful people have developed this ability and use it extensively. They see themselves achieving certain goals long before the actual achievement occurs. They imagine themselves closing that sale, buying that house, or scoring that touchdown, thus creating a self-fulfilling prophecy.

You need to devote only five to ten minutes each day to visualize yourself as a success in the future. The best time to practice the technique is when you are most relaxed—before going to sleep, before rising, after dinner, or whenever is best for you. Seek out a quiet place where you will not be disturbed. Then relax and visualize yourself achieving a certain goal: making an important speech, taking over the boss's job, moving into the $100,000-a-year salary bracket. Visualize all the details of the setting—the place, time, people involved, and so on. Imagine the way people will act and the things they will say.

Think of the pleasure you will derive from attaining that goal. Keep imagining it; see yourself attaining the goal, and see yourself feeling satisfied with the achievement. This is no idle daydream, but an honest attempt to convince yourself that you can attain your goals. You will then attain your goal because you are totally convinced you can do so.

NO FEAR OF FLYING

*The greatest mistake you can make is to be
continually fearing that you'll make one.*
—Elbert Hubbard

*A mistake is evidence that somebody tried to
accomplish something.*

Successful people believe they can succeed. They focus on the pleasure that comes from succeeding rather than on the misery that results from failing. For example, the successful real estate investor might say, "By buying a house and renting it to someone else, I could make X dollars each year and have a good long-term investment." The unsuccessful investor thinks like this: "If I use the money in the bank for the down payment on a house, I'll lose X dollars in interest each year and feel less secure." That fear of risk may result in standing still. The person who is willing to take some chances can attain a great measure of success, assuming he or she plans carefully.

Consider these two scenes in two small life insurance companies. Both companies are considering expanding their services by acquiring a multi-line insurance company.

A. Boyd Risks: I want to discuss with you the possible acquisition of Multi-Line Insurance. I'm not so sure we should acquire the company. We here at Slogro Insurance are doing all right just the way we are. I'm afraid something will go wrong. The costs are also too much for me.

Manager No. 1: But we could really use a multi-line carrier to expand our overall services. Mixing a life insurance and a multi-line firm together would enable us to offer our clients a wider product range. The two businesses would complement each other nicely.

A. Boyd: I know that, but what if Multi-Line isn't such a hot company?

Manager No. 2: We checked them out carefully, and their financial condition is very healthy. They are well managed, profitable, and expected to grow even without an acquisition or merger.

A. Boyd: But what if the acquisition doesn't work?

Manager No. 1: I'm sure there'll be some problems, but I think we could work them out.

A. Boyd: Costs are another concern. If we buy Multi-Line, our profits will be reduced for the next couple of years because of acquisition costs.

Manager No. 2: The profits of our current company might be reduced, but if we add in the profits from Multi-Line, we'll easily have a record year.

A. Boyd: Well, I just don't know. I hate to upset the apple cart, and we've been profitable for a number of years. Why should we change things?

I. L. Chancit: I want to discuss the possible acquisition of Multi-Line with you. I'm excited about what this business could do for us here at Rapidgro Insurance. An acquisition will require a lot of work, and no doubt we'll run into some problems, but I think we have to consider it.

Manager No. 1: Adding a multi-line carrier will complement our current services beautifully. The two firms combined can generate more business than either one alone.

I. L.: That's true. What do you think of Multi-Line as a company?

Manager No. 2: Our research shows they are financially sound and well managed. Expectations are for continued growth over the next several years and beyond.

I. L.: That is a very strong factor for an acquisition. How do you feel the acquisition would go?

Manager No. 1: Legally, there should be no problems. I'd advise that we keep the two companies fairly separate initially, but merge functions where suggested as a result of retirements. That should smooth the transition. There may be some minor problems with merging company philosophies and styles.

I. L.: I'm not worried about that. We can work those things out. Financially, we are going to have to borrow to acquire Multi-Line, but the long-term potential here is fantastic.

Manager No. 2: It will take us a few years to cover our acquisition costs, but profits will jump substantially in the first year and from there on out. It looks good financially.

I. L.: Well, I know we have a big challenge facing us, but I think we should go for it. This company will really skyrocket as a result of the acquisition.

A. Boyd Risks and I. L. Chancit took different approaches to the same situation. The overly cautious Boyd clearly did not want to take any chances. Disturbingly, he didn't even listen to the objective facts his staff presented in favor of the acquisition. As a result of his passing up an ideal opportunity, Boyd's company will not grow or prosper as it could have. While the company may still be profitable, its potential for success will be lessened.

I. L. Chancit took a positive approach to the situation. He was willing to take a risk if it seemed warranted. He listened to the information his staff presented and decided the acquisition would be worth the risk. I. L. is thinking more about the benefits of success than the consequences of failure. His position will lead to company growth and increased profitability.

If you have fears about setting high goals for yourself, deal with these fears as objectively as you can. Collect all the information you can pertaining to your decision and add up the pluses and minuses. If the evidence suggests that going forward will be profitable, then do so even if some risk is involved. If you wait for someone to sell you a $200,000 property for $40,000 with interest-free financing, you may have a long wait. Risk is inherent in any ambitious undertaking.

One way to dispel your fear of taking risks is to think of the good things that *will* happen, not of the bad things that *might* happen. Say, "I'm going to increase sales," not "I don't think I'll be able to make any more sales." When you look at your list of goals, avoid dwelling on the possible negative consequences; think only of the fame, money, and pleasure that success will bring.

JOINT OBJECTIVES

> *Lots of times you have to pretend to join a parade in which you're not really interested, in order to get where you are going.*
> —Christopher Morley

> *There are only two forces that unite men — fear and interest.*
> —Napoleon I

The focus in this book is on *your* objectives, but you can do a tremendous amount more with the help of others than you can by yourself. Attaining some of your objectives may require you to work with others. Your department may want to computerize its records systems, for instance, but to do this you need the assistance of the systems department. Or, to get venture capital to expand your business, you may seek out someone who wants to invest in your firm.

Conventional business settings offer many opportunities to accomplish *joint objectives* on your way to your own individual objectives. As the leader of a task force, team, or committee, for example, you can lead others toward a joint objective, proceed toward your own objective, *and* earn credit for the successful work of the team as a whole. Try forming your own team or task force to accomplish certain objectives. Have the members of your team "report" to you as the team leader. This will let the team members—who can be your peers, someone else's subordinates, or even those higher than you in another functional area of the company—see you in a leadership position. Remember, credit for the success of the group project will go to you as the person who took the initiative to get the team organized and who guided it through to its accomplishments.

Turn back now to the objectives you developed for yourself earlier. Ask yourself how you can turn them into joint objectives. The following directions will help you:

1. For each objective, make a list of the ways in which others

can assist you. Write down the names of individuals and the particular tasks they can perform in your behalf. Determine the cost, if any, associated with using the assistance of others. From your list select only those individuals whose assistance will be worth more than the associated costs.

2. Next obtain the actual assistance of those you have selected. If you've chosen members of your own staff, simply assign them to their new objective. But if you've also listed employees who do not report to you (peers or someone else's subordinates, for example), you will need to convince them and their bosses of the value of their assistance. Objectively tell them what they will gain (experience, for instance) by helping you attain your goals.

3. Establish yourself as the leader and as the focal point for all communications. Tell all team members what the joint objectives are and what their particular tasks are. Bring the team together regularly for updates, and circulate materials of interest to all team members.

4. When you have attained the joint objective, give out rewards—a note of appreciation, for example, or a public statement of praise—to each team member.

Joint objectives can be extremely beneficial, and they are, in fact, often a necessity. Remain always concerned about attaining your own objectives, but enlist the help of others whenever you can. This will help you and others to reach personal goals, and give everyone concerned an opportunity to see you in a leadership position.

3·

The Will to Do

ALWAYS MORE

Ah, but a man's reach should exceed his grasp.
— Robert Browning

Too low they build, who build beneath the stars.
— Edward Young

Many successful people have a deep, strong desire to attain their goals. This desire is the "will to do," a subconscious urge that keeps pushing you ever onward toward achievement. The subconscious drive for success is not clearly understood, but it is known that highly successful men and women have that strong urge to achieve.

People work hard if the rewards of their labor are great, but they don't try hard if the rewards are insufficient. According to this "equity concept" (developed by the psychologist J. Stacy Adams) people will expend, for example, four units of effort to attain something they value at four or more units, but they will not expend four units of effort for something that's worth only two units. Whether for money, status, learning, material goods, or a sense of achievement, successful people value some combination of rewards enough to make them drive hard to reach their goals. There is an equitable balance between the effort they put out and the rewards they receive; often the rewards exceed the effort.

Many successful people drive themselves hard simply because they enjoy their work. In other words, the task itself provides all the motivation they need. Money, status, and advancement are by-products of the enjoyable work. This is not to say that the highly successful are not interested in more wealth, fame, or status, but simply that these rewards are of secondary importance to accomplishing a task they greatly enjoy doing. The work itself is attractive to them beyond the external rewards they receive. That can be observed in many people who work beyond the usual retirement age. They do so not for wealth, but for sheer enjoyment of work itself. Highly successful people frequently perform their jobs with fervor, working long hours and sacrificing their leisure time to complete a particular task.

If you do not enjoy your job, chances are you will not be highly successful at it. If you're not satisfied with your work, you need to examine your interests and your abilities to see how they match up with your career, as discussed in Chapter 1.

A key component of long-term success is to keep aspiring to greater and greater things. You must never be content with things as they are, and never regard your own personal development as complete. When highly successful people accomplish one set of goals, they start working toward a new set immediately. If they acquire a certain skill, they try to perfect it, or they set out to acquire another skill. You sustain such motivation not only by concentrating on the rewards at the end of the road, but also by enjoying what you do.

You will often have others working for you in your quest for success, and your accomplishments will depend heavily on how effectively your people work. Therefore, you must be able to inspire them to do their best. Here's one technique you can use to inspire others to achieve more: delegate just enough responsibility to challenge your employees' abilities. People tend to work at their best when they are learning, developing, and feeling challenged on the job. When the job becomes routine, motivation wanes.

Let's say your secretary has mastered the skills of typing and filing. You could ask this secretary to do more work in the same amount of time (type more letters each day) or to improve the quality of the work (cut down on the number of typing errors). That may keep your secretary motivated for a while, but it is not nearly as effective as the motivation that would result from learning new skills and having new responsibilities.

As an alternative, you could encourage your secretary to learn basic accounting skills and to take some responsibility for the department budget. Or you can suggest that he or she learn to write computer programs and store department records and reports in the computer. These incentives are likely to sustain higher performance for a longer time.

When you give people additional responsibilities, be aware that there is a fine line between too much work and too little. Know how much each employee can do right now; then *gradually* increase that person's responsibilities. You'll be well on the way to inspiring your staff toward greater accomplishments if you realize that each employee has different desires and abilities.

Suppose that your secretary does learn to write computer programs. As a beginning project, he or she is supposed to write programs to generate your monthly reports, and you notice your secretary is struggling with this. It's time for you to step in, take an expert look over the employee's shoulder, and offer your assistance. After you get the programming problem solved, step out of the way and allow the secretary to do this work independently.

People work hard for different reasons. For some, the challenge of the job itself is enough. Others strive for money or material rewards. Some like the recognition or status the job might bring or the good feeling they get from accomplishments. Yet others are inspired by the opportunity to learn new skills. People want more of whatever it is that motivates them. Find out what the incentive is for your people, and provide more of it. This is discussed in more depth later in this chapter, but first let's talk about some incentives you can offer *all* of your employees.

GREAT EXPECTATIONS

The world has a way of giving what is demanded of it.
If you are frightened and look for failure and poverty, you will get
them, no matter how hard you try to succeed. Expect victory and you
make victory.
—Preston Bradley

Great hopes make great men.
—Thomas Fuller

Set your expectations high, but be realistic. Similarly, your expectations of others must be high. Successful people *expect* to succeed. They honestly believe they will accomplish difficult tasks, even those that others regard as impossible. And because of their high expectations, they accomplish much more than others who lack that conviction. If you firmly believe you will succeed, little will stop you from reaching your goal.

You'll find one good example of high expectations in the movie *Patton.* In one scene, all of the Allied generals were seated around a conference table discussing how to save a trapped British division that was being attacked on all sides. The generals were asked what they could do to save the trapped men. No one spoke up at first. Then one British general said he couldn't do anything. At that point, Patton said, "I can attack with three divisions within forty-eight hours." Now that is expecting success! Against tremendous odds, Patton moved his troops farther and faster than anyone in U.S. military history, and successfully liberated the trapped British troops.

Set high expectations whenever you can. Use phrases like these:

- "We will get the job done."
- "I see no problems that we can't handle."
- "You can count on us."
- "I have the team to get the job done."

Positive thinking is the mark of a winner. And win you will if you really believe in yourself and in those who work for you.

Your expectations of success are strongly influenced by the amount of control you feel you have over yourself. The more control you have, the more certain you can be of achieving success. Some individuals regard their lives as corks floating on the ocean. They hope the winds and currents will carry them into a safe harbor, but feel they are powerless to control their journey. Because of this perceived lack of control, they do not expect success and, therefore, do not attain it.

Other individuals, however, put a motor and rudder on the cork floating on the ocean. They realize the winds and currents are still there, but they are determined to control their course. They expect to succeed, and they usually do.

To what extent do you expect to succeed at the different things you do? How much control do you feel you have over the course of your life? How often do you say, "I can," instead of "I can't" when presented with a challenge? Remember that the enthusiasm and confidence you project will serve as a cue to others who are working for or with you toward attaining goals. If you expect failure, you will get failure. Expect success, and you will get success. Have an enthusiastic attitude toward the future. Say things like this:

- "I'm really excited about this new project."
- "This is going to be an excellent learning opportunity for all of us."
- "This is a great chance to show what we can do."

If you use phrases like these, the people who work with you will catch your excitement and achieve greater things. And that is exactly what you want them to do.

THE CONFIDENCE GAME

Sir Arthur Eddington, a British astronomer, was once asked: "Is it true, Sir Arthur, that you are one of the three men in the world who understands Einstein's theory of relativity?"
The astronomer appeared reluctant to answer.
"Forgive me," said his questioner, "I should have realized a man of your modesty would find such a question embarrassing."
"Not at all," said Eddington, "I was just trying to think who the third could be."

Skill and confidence are an unconquered army.
—George Herbert

Most successful people have confidence in themselves and in those who work for them. Such confidence is essential in a leader. Not many would follow you across a chasm if you said, "I don't think any of us can make it." You must be confident if you want to attain your intended goals, and you must transmit your confidence to others.

This does not mean, however, that your confidence must extend into areas where you have little expertise. If you pretend to be a master of everything, others will see that you overestimate your abilities and strengths, and underestimate your weaknesses. Their confidence in you will then vanish. You doubtless know people who are immensely talented at some things, but who confess to be all thumbs at other activities. This admission is disarming and sometimes endearing.

For example, one very talented speaker I know sometimes fumbles with the audiovisual equipment. He does this intentionally to endear himself to the audience. Everyone watches and identifies with him. As a result, by the time he starts to deliver his talk, the audience is already on his side.

Here's another example. A businessman was about to close a deal with an out-of-town executive. As the two drove around town, the host pretended he could not find the hotel where they were to close the deal. Then he had trouble finding a parking space. He knew his way around, of course, but he used this technique to disarm his visitor. When it came time to close the deal, he again exuded confidence. And he got precisely what he wanted.

Note that in these examples, the fumbled activity was outside the person's area of expertise. The speaker was in total command of his subject matter and delivery when he gave his talk. The executive was thoroughly confident of his facts, figures, and persuasive skills when he closed the deal. And so you should be with your area of expertise. Be extremely confident that no one could do it better and do not be afraid to show your confidence. If you admit to weaknesses, be sure they are unrelated to your area of expertise.

You can show self-confidence in a variety of ways. If someone pays you a compliment, acknowledge it politely. Don't act humble or make excuses. If you get a promotion, don't say, "I guess I was in the right place at the right time." Say instead, "I've worked long and hard, and I'm glad I made it." If someone compliments you on your sales presentation, do not say, "I've made some lucky sales lately." Instead say, "It went over well. I was really pleased with it." That is the talk of a successful person. It implies that you like yourself, and that you are a winner. And that is the image you want to project.

Self-confidence is an element in many success stories. Believe in yourself; recognize that you are not perfect, but that no one has ever been perfect. Your confidence must extend over your entire area of expertise. Limit your humility to activities outside that area. Accept compliments graciously, and build confidence in others who work for or with you.

DOING VERSUS THINKING

Well done is better than well said.
—Benjamin Franklin

*If you have something to do that is worthwhile doing,
don't talk about doing it, but do it. After you have done it, your
friends and enemies will talk about it.*
—George W. Blount

If there is one key to success, it is doing rather than simply thinking about doing. You must translate your hopes, aspirations, thoughts, and ideas into concrete actions if you want to receive any benefit from them. Otherwise you will have to enjoy your success, like Walter Mitty, in your daydreams—and no way are dreams more satisfying than the real thing.

Many people can put together good plans for success, but they fall short in implementing those plans. Some fail out of a simple fear of starting on a major activity that may require substantial time, effort, and skill. You may feel that the undertaking has little chance of success, so you put off doing it to avoid failure. The solution to this is to break the plan down into subgoals (see Chapter 2), each of which you have a reasonably good chance of attaining. This should bring your fear of failure under control.

Others fear that the plan will take too much time and work. If you tend to feel this way, make yourself think of the pleasure and enjoyment success will bring. Remember that success takes time and effort, but each step brings you closer to your long-range goal. And you will get rewards at each step along the way.

Yet other people fear success itself. They feel that the status, fame, and money associated with success will cause dramatic changes in their lives, and change always carries with it certain anxieties. If you feel this way, just remember that your life will change anyway, whether or not you become successful. Why not take charge of your life and make sure that the changes are for the best, instead of simply letting changes happen to you, not doing anything about them, and then attributing the outcome to bad luck. Wouldn't you rather sit in a mansion worrying about how to spend a million dollars than sit in a tiny apartment in a bad neighborhood wondering why you never made it? The choice is yours. By being a doer, by making things happen, you can control the changes that occur during the rest of your professional life.

Here's a final word of advice on taking action to ensure success: *Start immediately.* Don't postpone your plans until next year when "things will be better" or when you will "have more time." There is no better time than now. Think where you will be a year from now if you start today.

Brush aside any fears that you are too old to start. Many tremendous accomplishments were made late in life. Colonel Harlan Sanders started his Kentucky Fried Chicken empire when he was in his sixties and "retired." Ray Kroc purchased his first McDonald's restaurant when he was fifty-two. Many others have successes just like these. Plan for success throughout your life, including your retirement.

MOTIVATION

> *Some people think they are overworked because it takes them all day to do a three-hour job.*

Whether you're motivating yourself or others, you should use as many incentives as you can. Motivators include growth, learning, status, a sense of achievement, praise, money, and material rewards.

Some managers complain that they can do nothing to motivate their people. Rewards are controlled by company policy, they say, and they cannot control policy, so how can they reward people? Nothing could be further from the truth. Every manager has access to numerous motivators.

Say you want to get one of your employees to set up a computerized records system for your department. Your staff is already busy, so this project will be an add-on. How do you sell it? Easy. You offer whatever the chosen individual wants.

You would like I. Emma Student to handle the project. Emma, a recent college grad, is eager to learn and to broaden her skills. Sell her on the project by offering her what she wants: an opportunity to learn. Show her that the computerized records project will offer her an excellent way to learn about systems applications in a staff department. The result: Emma wants the project.

Or maybe you want Herman M. Grubber to take on the project (the "M" stands for Money). You tell Herman that the project is a way to earn extra money. If he successfully completes this project, he will get a higher performance appraisal rating and a greater salary increase, assuming he does not slip in other performance areas. Herman wants the project, thinking of the money involved.

Maybe the employee you want to do the job is I. Wanda Praise. Wanda needs recognition and praise more than anything else. Tell Wanda you have given a great deal of thought to choosing the best person for this project. Because of Wanda's special skills, you have chosen her. As the project progresses, you praise Wanda in front of others for her excellent work. And at the end of the project, you write her a letter of appreciation or give her a certificate of accomplishment.

These examples are, of course, overly simplified. Each employee is likely to be motivated by more than just one need. But you can show that completing the project could satisfy multiple needs. However, each individual will have some needs that are stronger than others, and these are the ones you should appeal to most. In order to do this, you must know and understand what your employees want. You might present a project in six different ways to six different people. That's okay, as long as the job gets done and the needs of your employees are satisfied.

Always be honest with your employees in situations like this. Never, never lie to them. If you tell Emma the project will be a learning experience, then it really must be a learning experience. If they do a good job on the project, Herman really must earn more money and Wanda really must receive the praise she deserves. Be candid with your employees, but make the project appeal to each individual. You, as a supervisor, are in a powerful position. You can get the job done, and you can make your people happy at the same time. To this end, use all the techniques you have at hand.

RUGGED DETERMINATION

If you get up one time more than you fall, you make it through.

To get through the longest and hardest journey, you need to take only one step at a time, but you must keep on stepping.

A good many of the most successful business leaders once faced hard times and even dismal failure, and the same thing will happen to you, perhaps, as you set out in pursuit of success. Keep in mind that it's okay to fail, but it's not okay to give up in the face of failure. What do you do if you get knocked down? Lie on the ground for the rest of your life? Of course not. You get right back up. In business—same thing. You fail at one thing; you try again or you try something else. But you don't give up. Ever.

Even if your failures greatly outnumber your successes, you can still achieve success. Here are two examples:

- You're looking for a job. You respond to a hundred ads and make a hundred personal contacts. Only ten of these contacts result in interviews. Of these ten, only two (1 percent of the total) result in acceptable job offers. That is a low probability of success, yet all you need is one acceptable offer to accomplish your objective.
- As an inventor, you tinker with hundreds of ideas for new products. Of these, only a few actually result in prototypes.

types. Eventually you relegate some of these prototypes to the scrap heap, but your efforts finally result in two successful patents, which bring you a high income. You reached your goal of developing a successful new product despite the number of failures you had along the way.

Each example makes an important point: it pays to keep trying. Don't be disheartened by failure; remain confident of your abilities; know that sooner or later you will succeed. And when you do attain your goal, remember that it was your skill and effort that caused your success — not luck.

In many ways, failures can enhance success. After failing at something, you may set out to acquire additional skills or knowledge in some area. Or you may become mentally or physically tougher to help you overcome future obstacles. Let's say you want your boss to approve a $50,000 expenditure for a new robot. You approach your boss and explain what you want. The boss is not convinced and says no. Now, you can do two things: give up or try again. If you give up, no way will you get the robot. If you try again, no way can you be any worse off than you already are.

You decide to try again. You reflect on your earlier failure and ask yourself how you could improve. You figure you did a poor job of selling your idea to the boss. After doing some research, you discover that the $50,000 robot could replace, through attrition, three employees whose salaries and benefits total $75,000 a year. And the robot could produce 20 percent more work than these employees, saving another $15,000 a year. Therefore, the company will save $40,000 a year *each year* the robot is used.

Armed with facts, charts, and figures, you make a terrific presentation to your boss. He now sees the idea in a different light, one of saving rather than expenditure. As a result, he reviews the matter with his boss. Eventually, you get the equipment. And you now have developed a new skill: making a dramatic and convincing presentation.

The important point here is that setbacks can lead you to develop new skills that increase your effectiveness. Whenever you experience a key failure, go through the following steps:

1. Identify the circumstances responsible for your failure—lack of a certain skill, for instance. Write down the things that caused the failure.
2. Ask yourself how you can improve. What additional skills, abilities, or information can you acquire to ensure success next time? Write these down.
3. Work to improve those areas. Ask for help from others wherever you need it.
4. Try again to do what you failed to accomplish earlier.
5. If this attempt fails, too, repeat steps 1 to 4 until you get the desired outcome. Remember that perseverance is essential for success.

4•

Lead the Way to Success

MODEL LEADERS

> *The final test of a leader is that he leaves behind him*
> *in other men the conviction and will to carry on.*
> —Walter Lippmann

> *If you command wisely, you'll be obeyed cheerfully.*
> —Thomas Fuller

Not everyone can be a leader. Some lack the ambition or interest; others lack the skills or abilities; and yet others simply never get a chance to put their leadership skills to use. Actually there are two kinds of leaders: those who supervise others, and those who are authorities or experts in some area but who do not supervise others. Both kinds of leadership are of interest to you in your quest for success, because leadership is often synonymous with success.

Many business careers, as you know, demand leadership in the form of direct supervision. This is true of corporate executives and small business entrepreneurs as well. The higher you advance, the more people you are likely to have working for you. In almost any field you'll have to direct others if you want to attain success. Your own achievement will be due largely to your own efforts, of course, but you will also have to rely on the efforts of those you supervise. How well you lead the way will determine how well they work. By leading them skillfully so that they achieve a great deal, you will ensure your own success. Remember always that a leader is someone people follow because they want to, not simply because they know he or she is the boss and has the power to fire them.

What does it take to be an effective leader? Research has shown that most good leaders have certain abilities and skills. If we condense and combine the results of the various studies, we come up with eight critical skills:

1. **Planning**—Determining the best course of action to take and mapping out a plan for getting where you want to go.
2. **Organizing**—Classifying, categorizing, pulling things together, making sense out of nonsense.
3. **Directing**—Giving specific instruction and guidance to others.
4. **Communicating**—Listening, speaking, writing, and passing information up, down, and laterally.
5. **Analyzing and evaluating**—Studying people, things, and information and making judgments about what you learn.
6. **Making decisions**—Choosing the best of several alternatives.
7. **Setting and maintaining high standards**—Setting a good example, setting high goals and expectations.
8. **Cultivating good human relations**—Motivating others and being sensitive to their needs.

In other words, successful leadership requires a diverse set of skills. Though anyone can make decisions, a leader must learn to make the right decision with limited information and time in a highly complex area, and that is another matter altogether. That is where you separate the successful from the not so successful.

One way to understand how the highly successful demonstrate these skills is to choose and study a role model. Choose someone whom you greatly admire and who has demonstrated his or her ability as an effective leader. This can be someone who works, or who once worked, in your company, or you can choose someone who works elsewhere but whom you often see in action. Make sure that your role model is a business leader. Don't choose Abraham Lincoln or the incumbent President of the United States. They undoubtedly demonstrate splendid leadership skills, but their experience is too far removed from yours because their field is government and politics, not business. No matter how much you admire them, their world is not your world. You'll learn more from the CEO in your company or from the vice-president of research and development of another firm whom you see regularly at meetings, conferences, and civic events.

Once you have chosen an appropriate role model, observe him or her carefully at every possible opportunity. Later, analyze this person's leadership abilities one by one, using the eight-item list provided here.

Your role model undoubtedly has the first ability on the list—planning. What must he or she plan? Can you see evidence of planning in the work place? Is it obvious to you that workers know exactly what they are supposed to do and exactly where they are headed? Is this due to your role model's planning ability?

Move on to the second item on the list—organizing—and look for evidence in the work place of your role model's organizing ability. Then go on to directing, communicating, and so forth until you have thoroughly analyzed this person's leadership skills.

From now on, keep your eye on your role model, looking always for evidence of those eight vital leadership skills and for ways in which you can emulate your model by improving your own control of those skills. By changing your own behavior to become more like your role model, you increase your leadership effectiveness.

TOTALLY ABSORBED

I am wondering what would have happened to me if some fluent talker had converted me to the theory of the eight-hour day and convinced me that it was not fair to my fellow workers to put forth my best efforts in my work. I am glad that the eight-hour day had not been invented when I was a young man. If my life had been made up of eight-hour days I do not believe I could have accomplished a great deal.
—Thomas A. Edison

Work is often the father of pleasure.
—Voltaire

What is the source of the magnetism that all great leaders possess? This magnetism seems to arise from the leader's excitement about and intense commitment to the job. Successful people, for the most part, thoroughly enjoy their work. They *want* to do this job, and others often perceive their enthusiasm as magnetism.

If you are asking yourself how anyone could possibly get excited about work, and if you feel no excitement about your job, you'd better ask yourself if you're in the wrong field (see Chapter 1). When you are appropriately matched up with your job, the work at hand will be something you enjoy doing. You would probably do this even if you didn't have to. If your work is a source of pleasure to you, your enjoyment of it will come through to others. Even when you simply talk about your work, people will sense your enthusiasm—or lack of it. Also, if you have that kind of enthusiasm, others will perceive you as a leader in your field—in other words, as a success.

Imagine you know two senior accountants. They have the same job responsibilities, but totally different attitudes toward their work. You have lunch one day with senior accountant number one, Noah Spirit.

"Noah," you ask, "how are things going at the office?"

"Oh, same old stuff," mumbles Noah. "It's never any different. We just do the same things over and over."

"Don't you enjoy your work, Noah?" you ask.

"Oh, it's all right, I guess. I have to have a job. But I really look forward to the end of the day, and I find it hard to get up in the mornings."

"What specifically don't you like?"

"The work is boring. I never know what to do with myself, and my boss, well, he's no help. I just guess it's part of working for the XYZ Company."

On another day you talk with senior accountant number two, Tom X. Citement.

"Well, Tom," you ask, "how are things going at the office?"

"Great!" Tom replies. "I'm working on a really interesting project on health care cost containment. Did you know that twenty percent of the health care costs are related to over-charges for the same products or services that are provided cheaper elsewhere? And we're really getting a handle on how to identify, understand, and contain the costs. It'll have a big payoff for the company."

"Sounds interesting," you say. "What else are you working on?"

"Well, we have a couple of fascinating projects coming on stream. One involves a new accounting process for evaluating company profits. Our executives are really interested to see if this works better than the current accounting system. Another project involves . . ."

You get the idea. Tom creates his own excitement by the en-thusiasm he shows for his work. Noah comes across as a loser, not a leader. Who would be the more fascinating luncheon guest? Who would you rather work with? Work for? You would likely prefer Tom. You'd rather get caught up in his excitement than be dragged down into Noah's doldrums. Remember that both men have the same job, and yet one is excited and the other is bored.

This is a good time to ask yourself how you describe your work to others. When you talk about your work to your friends, do you use words like "boring" and "all right"? Are you the Noah Spirit type? Or do you find yourself repeating words like "interesting" and "fascinating," as Tom X. Citement does? The excitement you express will affect others who work for and with you. They will either share your excitement and become enthusiastic, or they'll share your depression and sink into despair. And similarly, those above you will perceive you either as a winner who wants to succeed or as a loser who has given up trying. It all depends on how much enthusiasm you feel, and show, for your work.

Can you act enthusiastic even if you're bored? Only to a certain extent. Suppose you say to a friend, "How's your job going?" The friend, in a monotone, says, "Okay, I guess," and shrugs. Even though the words indicate one thing, the voice and the body language tell you that your friend is bored with the job. It'll be the same way with you if you try to fake enthusiasm: the boredom will probably come through, giving the lie to your words. If you want others to believe that you're involved in and excited about your career, then you must really feel that way. Then you'll create your own enthusiasm.

But, you say, what if my job really is boring, and the only thing I can do is *act* enthusiastic about it? If there's no excitement in your work, you'll have to create some. Take on or develop new projects or responsibilities that you find exciting. Your boss will let you get involved in other things, particularly if you sell your idea enthusiastically and show how it will pay off. Read up on a new subject. Master a new skill. Devise techniques or work practices that are more effective than the ones you have been using. Then implement your new technique. Generate your own excitement.

When you want something badly and deeply, that feeling heightens your motivation and your determination to attain that goal. Everything else seems to diminish in importance when you concentrate your energies in one direction. You can accomplish more than you would ever imagine, and others will get caught up in your excitement. Don't wait for excitement to come up and introduce itself. Create some of your own and watch the results.

TRAILBLAZING

> *It isn't the common man at all who is important; it's the uncommon man.*
> —Lady Nancy Astor

> *If you want to succeed, you should strike out on new paths rather than travel the worn paths of accepted success.*
> —John D. Rockefeller

To lead others, you must set yourself apart from your peers. You might be brighter or more creative. You may work harder, manage people more effectively, get better results. Whatever you do, you'll have to do it significantly better than those around you if you want to get the next available leadership position. Those making promotional decisions want the best person they can get so you'd better become the best.

Acquire whatever skills, knowledge, or technical expertise you currently lack, and make others aware that you now have these new talents. Let the boss know of your extra effort to learn. Mention that you can put your new skills to their best use in your next job, the one you aspire to. That helps solidify the link between what you have and what you want. And it sets you a few steps ahead of the others.

If new skills will not set you apart from others, then try something else. Work longer hours, take on more projects, provide more ideas, be a better manager. Look at yourself honestly and evaluate your competition realistically. Keep improving your performance in each area until you have put some distance between yourself and your peers. That will ensure that you stand out in front of the crowd.

Perhaps the single best way to get a promotion is simply to convince your superiors that you are the best person for the job. Make sure they know that failure to promote you further would be a mistake, that the company will lose by not taking advantage of your abilities. And a job does not have to be vacant when you start campaigning for it. You can do this any time you're ready. To convince your superiors of your suitability, you need to:

1. Know what experience, knowledge, and skills the job requires.
2. Convince the decision-makers that you meet or exceed these requirements.
3. Convince the decision-makers that you have significantly more to offer than other candidates do.

Step 1 requires only a bit of homework. Study the job description and any job ads the company has used. Talk with incumbents. List all the information you can collect. Step 2 is a bit more difficult, for here you have to do a good job at selling. Present your case in a straightforward way. Even if the job is now filled, you may convince someone that you should be next in line. Request a meeting with the decision-maker and do the following:

- Tell the decision-maker you would like to discuss future job opportunities.
- Set up and conduct the meeting in a nonthreatening way. Do not request a final decision at your initial meeting; selection and promotion do not work that way.
- Do not make the decision-maker agree with you each step of the way. Avoid saying things like, "Don't you think I'm qualified?" That makes people uncomfortable or invites a no rather than a yes answer. Instead, make statements that can be challenged, but if not challenged, imply agreement. For example, you might say, "I trust you will agree my knowledge of this and that greatly exceeds what the job requires." If the decision-maker does not challenge you, that may indicate passive agreement.

In presenting your credentials, do not be intimidated if the job requires six years of experience and you have only five. Those job requirements are only preferences, and no candidate is likely to meet every one of them. Instead, explain why your five years' experience is the equivalent of ten years. That is the best way to counteract a possible deficiency.

If your interviewer does not ask you to describe your background, take the initiative by saying something like this: "I'm sure you would like to know how my background can benefit your company. Do you mind if I describe it to you?" Most interviewers will agree to this, for this is what they want to probe in an interview. Once you have the ball, explain step by step how you meet or exceed each job requirement. Emphasize how your skills, abilities and experience will affect bottom-line results. Cite key achievements from the past to support your case.

During the interview, do not restrict yourself to seeking an existing job. Too often people think only of currently available positions; they forget that jobs can be created or combined with others, as the situation demands. Take the opportunity to create a new job for yourself. Plan this ahead of time and sell the advantages of the new position to your interviewer. Once again, emphasize the bottom-line results the company will obtain by creating this new job and choosing you to fill it. If you are logical and persuasive, you might wind up with a lot more than the company initially planned to offer you—if they planned on offering you anything.

Many job candidates feel all they have to do is convince the interviewer they meet the job requirements; then they believe the battle will be over. Remember, however, that others might meet the job requirements. These individuals are also in the running and that is why step 3 is needed. This is where you must set yourself apart from these other candidates. If you know who your competitors are, never denigrate them by saying, "George can't do this. Bill doesn't know anything about this," and so on. Such a negative approach is likely to make a poor impression on the interviewer. Instead emphasize your own qualifications. Say things like this:

- "I have a year's worth of marketing experience in addition to my sales background, unlike many other people in the field."
- "I feel that my particular knowledge of computer applications sets me apart from most professionals in finance."
- "My national leadership in the ABC Professional Association has given me additional exposure most people in my area have not had."

Even if the job does not require marketing experience, computer knowledge, or involvement in a professional association, the fact that you have these strengths, whereas others do not, sets you apart from them. The interviewer will remember you have this additional experience when it comes time to make a decision. If all other things are equal, this could be the deciding factor in your favor. Any extra experience or skills you have make you stand out from the others.

You can set yourself apart from the group in other ways as well. You can make yourself stand out, for example, by having a more impressive office than others on your own job level. Never mind that it's the same size as everyone else's. Just find yourself a larger, better-quality desk, more elegant chairs, and more impressive pictures. Show people that you are different in a positive way. Create an impression that you are someone of high status and aspiration. Make it clear that you're a cut above other people.

The process of setting yourself apart extends to the way you dress, too. All businesses have certain dress conventions, but there is always room for personal distinction. If all the executives in your company wear dark suits and you want to be an executive, then by all means wear a dark suit. But your peers may also wear dark suits, so how can you set yourself apart? Certainly not by wearing bright checks and an orange blazer. That is different, but in the wrong direction. However, you could add a gold tie clasp or place a silk handkerchief in your jacket pocket. These touches are in keeping with the conservative dress code of the company, but differentiate you from your peers. You will be different, but in a way that will make you look the part of the person who gets promotions.

Perhaps you have heard of W. Clement Stone, the founder and chairman of Combined Insurance of Chicago. Stone, the foremost advocate of the "positive mental attitude," has two well-known trademarks: he always wears a bow tie, and he sports a pencil-thin mustache. These touches make him unique in appearance. Now, bow ties and mustaches might be too avant-garde for some corporations, but they have effectively set Stone apart from others. People perceive him as a very distinctive man. You might be able to find a trademark that will work well for you.

Successful people blaze their own trails to success; they don't trudge along the same road everyone else uses. What do most people do, for example, when they hear that certain stocks are a great investment? They watch the newspapers, see those stocks continue to go up, and then decide to buy. But the time to buy was before the big increase in stock values, not afterward. By the time most people decide to invest, it's too late; the stock has already peaked and is now on the decline. The highly successful investors are the ones who anticipated the rise and bought the stocks before they went up in value. Granted it took foresight and courage to step out in front of everyone else and take a chance on those new stocks, but successful people are the ones who have the foresight and the courage to explore new areas.

Blazing your own trail to success means not being content with things as they are. If you're always searching for better and newer ways to earn money or to do your job better, chances are you've got what it takes to be a trailblazer. Remember, though, that refusing to be contented should fill you with a desire to make your life better; it should *not* make you depressed and miserable. Attaining great success requires intelligence, perseverance, ability, high standards, and a strong urge to attain difficult goals. The strategy you map out for yourself may at times be less than perfect, but with the constant desire to improve, you will have more successes than failures. If you have the courage to step out in front, if you are not content with the status quo, you already have the makings of a leader. Now you have to take things in hand and make success happen to you.

MAKING THINGS HAPPEN

There are three kinds of people who work for organizations:
1) Those who make things happen
2) Those who watch things happen
3) Those who try to figure out what the hell happened.

To be is to do.
—Albert Camus

To do is to be.
—Jean-Paul Sartre

Successful people tend to be the center of activity, the focal point around which things happen. The actual work may be done by subordinates, but no one doubts that the energy, direction, and control behind the accomplishments emanates from that one center. Successful people are the ones you go to when you need to get results. They make things happen, and they get credit for doing so. Others want to share their attention and control. How can you become a person who makes things happen? You can undertake a number of activities.

Be an Expert

Become highly knowledgeable in your specialty. Be the most expert accountant, programmer, mechanical engineer, or middle manager. Others will seek your advice when they want to do things correctly, because they know you are the best source of information they have.

When you've mastered your own specialty area, keep going. Master another area, then a third and a fourth, until you know all the ins and outs of the company, including areas you're not responsible for. Get to know the people in other departments, divisions, and even regions. Learn how their operations run. More and more people will seek your counsel, and the reputation you build will increase your control over your future.

A word of caution, however. Don't become known as the expert in company gossip and rumors. That may win friends but it will not increase your prestige. Stick to company operations.

Be a High Achiever

Take on more work and deliver good results. Become known as the person who always gets the job done—efficiently, expertly, and on time. This enhances your importance to the company and enhances your reputation as an expert. You'll be "promoted" before you actually move into a better job. Executives will see you as the high achiever who always comes through, the person who takes on more work and delivers bottom-line results. That can lead to additional career opportunities for you.

Lead a Supereffective Team

Hire the best subordinates you can find. (You'll find tips on hiring a competent staff in Chapter 10.) See to it that your subordinates have greater competence and knowledge, work better together, and work harder than anyone else's team. Motivate them to deliver the best possible results. They'll earn respect for being part of a successful group, and as their leader you'll get plenty of credit for their successful efforts.

Be Gregarious

Talk to people on all levels of the company. Get to know the maintenance crew and the company mechanics as well as the vice-presidents. Show that you're interested in them as individuals, not just as employees. Don't limit yourself to asking them if they've finished clearing the storage areas or repairing the trucks. Ask about them as people: How was your vacation? How's the softball team doing? I see you've got a new car. How do you like it? Never be overly familiar, of course, and avoid personal questions, but do talk to people every chance you get.

Don't confuse gregariousness with office politics, however. Granted many people go that route, but if you choose to follow them, do so at your own risk. Playing politics means, in a nutshell, currying favor with those in power: cultivating close personal relations with key executives, playing golf with the boss, and often playing one person off against another to gain the favor of the powerful. This sort of thing is useful only as long as the people whose favor you're currying remain in power; once they move on, you may find yourself in the bad graces of those who replace them. Perhaps an even worse result of playing politics is that your tactics will be very obvious to almost everyone in the organization, and you will very quickly lose their respect.

5·
Successful Leadership Techniques

LEAD BY COMPETENCY

> *Knowledge is power.*
> —Thomas Hobbes

> *The winds and waves are always on the side of the*
> *ablest navigators.*
> —Edward Gibbon

Earlier you were introduced to eight critical abilities a successful manager must have: the ability to plan, organize, direct, communicate, analyze, make good decisions, maintain high standards, and cultivate positive human relations. Until now, however, not much has been said about another aspect of leading others, and that is technical competency. Your technical competency depends on how much you know about the area you are managing. Even if you are the greatest natural leader in the world, you will falter if you lack technical competence.

You must have a good working knowledge of every area you oversee. A manager of programming operations, for example, may not know how to debug each computer program his department runs across, but he or she must know a great deal about computer operations and programming. Otherwise it will be difficult to provide direction to the staff, make decisions, and set goals. Similarly, a hospital manager need not be able to diagnose and evaluate patients. Others will perform that specialty function. But the administrator who doesn't understand the health care delivery process and the services that are available will be in big trouble. Content knowledge is vital, especially if you have experts working for you.

A great switch in the competencies is required when you move into management from a nonmanagement position. Before assuming a leadership position, you might have established competence in programming, mechanics, or accounting, but now, in addition to competency in a specific content area, you need managerial competency. Knowledge in the content area is not as critical now as it once was. Mechanics may still enjoy getting their hands dirty, but they'll need different skills when they move into management.

Your effectiveness as a leader is judged partly on the basis of your management skills and technical knowledge, but your work habits and personal conduct will also determine your effectiveness in leading others. These things set the tone and establish a style for others to follow.

To gain further insight into how your work habits and personal conduct affect your competency as a leader, pretend for a moment that you are judging the effectiveness of others as leaders. Assume you know nothing about these people other than what you read about them in the following paragraphs. Which person would impress you most as a leader? Which one would you follow?

Leader A is a conscientious, hardworking individual. He always gets to work on time and keeps longer hours than most of the staff. His pattern is to arrive early, stay late, and take work home. Although he's a workaholic, he has a variety of outside interests.

Leader B arrives and leaves at about the same time as the clerical staff. On occasion, he will work late or take work home, but that doesn't happen often. Leader B seems to enjoy his job, but he doesn't believe it's worth any extra effort. He sometimes sneaks out early on Friday afternoons and very often takes extended lunch hours.

Who impresses you more as a leader, A or B?

Leader C is careless about his dress and appearance. His suit is sometimes soiled or wrinkled, his hair is not combed at times, and on occasion his shirt is partially out of his pants or his collar is turned up in the back. Leader C is as careless about his office as he is about his clothes. Books and papers are strewn everywhere, and he has difficulty locating materials.

Leader D's appearance is always neat. His clothes are clean and well pressed, and his hair is always well groomed. His office is tidy, with current work organized in neat piles. He has easy access to all his materials, which he has organized in files and bookcases.

Who impresses you more as a leader, C or D?

Leader X takes a great many phone calls from her family and friends during the work day. Her outside interests also take up a lot of company time. Her conversations about a recent party or vacation sometimes last longer than they should. And she is often observed reading novels during office hours.

Leader Y always seems to be busy. When you walk past her office, she is always writing or meeting with others, and she's completely absorbed in whatever she's doing. Her personal conversations never last very long; she usually ends them by saying, "I need to get back to work." That seems abrupt at times, but others respect her because of her constant good work.

Who impresses you more as a leader, X or Y?

The choices are easy ones. Certainly, Leaders A, D, and Y impress you much more than their counterparts. The important point is that personal appearance and behavior enter largely into your judgment of these people as leaders, even though you know absolutely nothing about their technical competence. Those who conducted themselves professionally impressed you more than the others. If people are sloppy in personal appearance, you infer that they are sloppy in their work. If they work very hard, you conclude they are going places. In other words, there is a connection between personal conduct and perceived leader effectiveness.

What impression does your personal conduct make on others? Do you work longer and harder than anyone around you, particularly your subordinates? Do you waste company time talking about your personal life? Or do you make use of every minute for company work? Is your appearance neat and professional? Or are you careless or unconcerned about how you look? Such details affect the opinions others have of you, especially those who work for you. Your subordinates also are likely to pick up your attitude; if you are careless, you will have a careless staff. If you arrive late or leave early, your staff will do likewise. If you waste company time on personal matters, so will your staff. To be an effective leader, you must set the best possible example and maintain it all the time.

Let's talk for a minute about that important distinction between being a leader and being merely a boss. Bosses are those who, by virtue of their position in a company, are responsible for supervising others; they may or may not be leaders. Those whose behavior places them in a commanding role are leaders, regardless of their official position in a company; in other words, they may or may not be bosses. Everyone knows who the leaders are, but finding out who the bosses are may require an organizational chart. If you are a boss or aspire to be one, make sure you are also a leader. You will need true leadership if you hope to gain advancement, respect, and status. Establish absolute competency in your field and then learn about other relevant fields. Gain as much knowledge of your content area as you possibly can. Maintain the highest standards of personal conduct and behavior. Success as a leader will likely follow.

TOUGH STUFF

A good employee likes a hard boss. I don't mean a
nagging boss or a grouchy boss. I mean a boss who insists on things
being done right and on time, a boss who is watching things closely
enough so that he knows a good job from a poor one. Nothing is
more discouraging to a good employee than a boss who is not on the
job, and who does not know whether things are going well or badly.
—William Feather

Success is the sum of detail. It might perhaps be
pleasing to imagine oneself beyond detail and engaged only in great
things, but as I have often observed, if one attends only to great
things and lets the little things pass, the great things become little:
that is, the business shrinks.
—Harvey S. Firestone

Your success as a leader will depend partly on the standards
you set and the consistency with which you maintain those
standards. If you ignore minor errors, your staff will continue
to make them, because they know it is acceptable. Careless-
ness about small errors will soon become standard operating
procedure. On the other hand, if you insist that the final product be perfect, your staff will strive to make fewer mistakes. The
leader sets the tone of the work place in countless ways, and
people respond to the cues their leader provides. The final
product you turn out is determined by the standards you set.
You can't blame others for sloppy results if you tolerate careless work. High standards firmly maintained most often result
in a better product.

Being a leader doesn't mean criticizing, nagging, or losing
your temper when things are not perfect. To be a tough leader
you must have high expectations for yourself and others, and
you must refuse to tolerate poor work, but you can still be
friendly and likable. You can insist on excellent performance
and still be courteous and tactful. But your standards must be
high if you hope to obtain super results. Here are just a few
things you can do to become a tough leader:

Confront Problems Squarely

If one of your subordinates is not doing a job properly, confront the problem immediately. Don't ignore it and don't make excuses for the employee. Take the person aside and do whatever coaching is required to bring his or her performance up to standard. That's the only way to get better work; the problem will not go away by itself.

If you ignore such problems, your employees will conclude that (1) you don't care if they goof up; (2) you are not sharp enough to know they're making mistakes; or (3) you have low standards and expectations for them. All of these conclusions make you look bad to your employees, your peers, and your boss. And, most important, you cannot obtain quality results with poor performance.

The poor performer may be as uncomfortable with the situation as you are. Employees may have personal problems that are affecting their work, or they might have skill deficiencies they are unaware of. You may even discover that some people are mismatched in their current jobs. You can help solve all of these problems only if you confront them. When you know what's causing the poor performance, you can correct the problem professionally, without hurting the person's feelings or pride.

Here are eight steps you can take to correct a performance problem:

1. Carefully document the employee's job behavior. Note very specifically where the performance has fallen short and collect specific examples to back up your judgment. Make sure you record objective, job-related actions that are under the employee's control, not subjective opinions.
2. After accumulating sufficient performance data, schedule a private meeting with the employee.
3. At the meeting, describe the employee's performance deficiency as objectively as you can and explain how his or her actions contrast with the job requirements. Indicate that improvement is needed. Ask the employee to explain the reasons for the poor performance. Do not present explanations yourself; stick to objective facts.

4. Reach agreement with the employee on what he or she will do to correct the problem. Express confidence in the employee's ability to improve.
5. Continue to document employee performance for several weeks after the meeting.
6. Reward the employee for improved performance.
7. Repeat steps 1 through 4, if you have to, but if the problem persists after the third repetition, give the employee a written warning.
8. If the employee cannot or will not correct the problem, your options are to transfer, demote, or terminate him or her.

Ask Questions

Another means of establishing yourself as a tough leader with high standards is to refuse to take anything for granted. If you're reviewing a proposal, budget, or plan that someone else has written, ask questions and probe for details. Make sure the assumptions behind the plan are solid and that the person doing the selling can defend them. In short, you can show tough leadership by refusing to be an easy sale. Ask tough questions. Suggest alternatives that the person may have failed to consider. But always phrase your suggestions in a positive way, like this:

- "Wouldn't it be better if you did this or that?"
- "Have you considered this or that possibility?"
- "Where did the figures on line ten come from?"
- "I think you will find that the correct total is $102,000, not $100,200."

Check and verify all information given to you. If the phone bill seems too high and you do not recall making those long-distance calls, look into the situation further. Do not accept this because it is the company's money and not your own. Investigate; gather all the information you need to resolve the problem. If your staff forwards reports or expense statements to you for approval, verify the information you are uncertain of. Ask all the questions that need to be asked. This will establish you as a person with high standards and expectations. Your staff will behave likewise. Constructive comments and questions let others know you pay attention to detail and expect good results. Errors or lack of detail will not get by you. You expect things to be correct, right down to the smallest detail. This style of management is associated with success, not failure. Be positive, helpful, and open-minded, but pursue things until they are satisfactory.

Send Out Error-Free Reports

When you prepare written materials, make sure they are error-free before you distribute them. If others see typos, misspellings, or bad grammar in a report that has your name on it, they'll draw negative conclusions about you, not about your typist. They'll think you're not smart enough to catch errors or that you just don't care. Either way, you'll have made a poor impression. Examine all materials that carry your name, and revise them until they're perfect. This will encourage others to be vigilant when they prepare materials for you. If they know you're going to proofread and correct their work, they'll make sure it's in good shape before they send it on to you. They'll see you as a tough leader with high standards.

Demand a Perfect Product

Don't let substandard products get past you. If the product doesn't meet your standards, don't pass it on. Require your people to do it over or revise it until it meets your tough standards. If you demand high-quality products and encourage others to demand high quality, then high quality is what you'll get.

Be Prompt

A tough leader must set and maintain high standards with regard to tardiness, extended lunch hours, and long coffee breaks. Of course, you'll take a two-hour lunch break occasionally, but don't establish a pattern of tardiness, early departures, and long lunch hours and breaks, and don't let your subordinates do so either. Set a proper example yourself and demand promptness in others. It's one additional way to be fair but firm.

Some readers may regard proofreading reports, verifying information, and checking for quality as nitpicking. It is. But every top-notch leader is a nitpicker. In fact, the failure to nitpick almost always results in a poor-quality product. For example, suppose that you buy a new car. The shiny paint is pitted within a few months, and the gas gauge is inaccurate. Wouldn't you have appreciated a nitpicking assembly-line inspector? Or let's say you're hospitalized because a technician switched your blood sample with someone else's, resulting in a misdiagnosis. Wouldn't you have appreciated more care and attention to detail? Don't you wish the lab supervisor had been a nitpicker?

Tough standards are needed in all endeavors, not just checking automobiles or handling blood samples. The products and services you turn out are important. Your constant vigilance will lead to a higher-quality product that will benefit everyone. Because you're a leader, it's up to you to set standards for your unit and see to it that they are maintained. Change your management style if necessary. Toughness will help you attain success.

IN CONTROL

Immense power is acquired by assuring yourself in your secret reveries that you were born to control affairs.
—Andrew Carnegie

The question "Who ought to be the boss?" is like asking "Who ought to be the tenor in the quartet?" Obviously the man who can sing tenor.
—Henry Ford

Leaders have a strong desire to control, to be in charge of people, activities, and programs. They enjoy directing others, making important decisions, altering the course of events, and being accountable for large areas of responsibility. Controlling events is satisfying to a leader.

You can't *learn* to want to control the destinies of others. Either you want that deep down inside or you don't. If you do want to control great enterprises but are having difficulty accomplishing this, you can take certain steps to increase the amount of control you have.

Convince Yourself

If you firmly believe that you are destined to manage large-scale enterprises, to control many people and activities, that compelling belief will help you gain control. But first you must convince yourself that this is something you are capable of doing. That conviction must be your starting point. If you don't believe in yourself, you will never gain control.

In your daydreams you should imagine yourself in a powerful role. See yourself as the president of the company or a successful entrepreneur. Set out to make your daydreams a reality. Tell yourself each evening that you *will* control things, that you *can* do the job effectively. Envisioning yourself in control is an important step toward getting what you want.

Act the Part

If you want to be in charge of many others, then behave in such a way as to convince people that you are a take-charge leader. Maintain high work standards, dress and talk like an executive, associate with other executives; in short, act the part in all your day-to-day activities. Others will see you as an executive, regardless of whether or not you actually hold the position.

Just as an actor can play a part convincingly, you can convince others you are a powerful leader. This is not deceptive. Quite the opposite. If you are observant enough to notice what a leader does, says, and is, then you understand the position and can be that way yourself, by acting similarly. After a while this becomes the real you. You are no longer acting decisive to play a role, but you *are* decisive.

If you behave like a person holding the position you aspire to, you will likely become that kind of person. And when others are looking for a leading executive, they will look to you because you act and look like an executive. More important, you may have the control and status of an executive before you ever get there if you behave like one. You will increase your importance and influence before the promotion occurs. Acting the part has many such benefits.

Request Assistance

Another way to gain control is to request assistance of others. Send out memos asking others for their suggestions on some topic of current concern. There is no reason why you cannot include those higher in rank in such a survey. Tell them you need their advice and suggestions on this matter. Accept full responsibility for combining the suggestions and acting on the results. This may lead to a decision that will affect many others, and you'll get credit for it because your effort got those results.

Increase Your Sphere of Control

Another control technique is to seek responsibility beyond your own work unit. In particular, pay attention to those areas no one is responsible for. Perhaps your company needs to provide additional training for sales representatives or needs to add a marketing support function to its sales department. Use these excellent opportunities to expand your sphere of control. Go forward with proposals to train sales reps or supplement the sales department. Show how these new activities will attain important goals.

If a neighboring work unit is without a manager due to a retirement, transfer, or promotion, propose that this work unit be merged with your area, with you in charge. Point out how that would save money. Having more responsibilities and a bigger staff will enhance your stature in the organization. People will see that you are growing in importance.

Let Others Know Your Career Goals

If you want more control and a higher level position, you must make others aware of this. It is surprising how many people fail to do this. Such people may lack the assertiveness to tell others what they want. They hope that higher-level jobs will fall at their feet, but that's not the way it works. You should tell others what type of position you want and convince them that you are the best person for the job. That will enhance your chances of receiving the position.

Invite Yourself to the Party

Another way of expanding your control is to get involved in other people's responsibilities. This is an assertive means of expanding your control, so use a great deal of tact here. If you hear about a report that is of interest to you, but that you did not receive, call the person who wrote it and ask for a copy. Read it and send a written response to the author. Make helpful suggestions or comments on the subject matter. This gets you involved in the process, and the author may invite you to subsequent meetings on the topic or include you on the mailing list for subsequent memos. As a result, you have expanded your sphere of control.

Similarly, if you find out about a meeting that you were not invited to, call the person who is chairing the meeting and ask if you can attend. Tell this person you're interested in this subject and explain how it relates to your responsibilities and interests. Chances are you'll be allowed to attend. During and after the meeting, provide helpful comments and offer to take some productive steps. This will help you broaden your scope of responsibility.

TIME FOR SUCCESS

*Time is the one thing that can never be retrieved.
One may lose and regain a friend; one may lose and regain money;
opportunity once spurned may come again; but the hours that are
lost in idleness can never be brought back to be used in gainful
pursuits. Most careers are made or marred in the hours after
supper.*
—C. R. Lawton

*Don't be fooled by the calendar. There are only as
many days in the year as you make use of. One man gets only a
week's value out of a year while another man gets a full year's value
out of a week.*
—Charles Richards

As you become increasingly more successful, the demands on
your time will increase until there will not seem to be enough
time to get everything done. Some people sacrifice certain goals
at this point, because, they say, "I don't have time for it." A
much better response to time pressure is to readjust your
schedule to make more time available for achieving your goals.
You can accomplish this in several ways.

Use Your Time Efficiently

You must make efficient use of nearly every available minute. If
you have only ten or fifteen minutes to spare before a meeting,
do not conclude that the time is too short to get anything done.
Instead of sitting idly, think of something you have to do that
will take only a few minutes. Perhaps you could read some material in your in-basket, organize your desk or files, plan tomorrow's activities, or write a memo. If you waste these ten- to
fifteen-minute periods each day, the loss can amount to an hour
each week, and over the course of a year it will amount to some
fifty or sixty hours.

Some people complain that their time is limited, yet they
spend hours in unproductive activities—watching television,
gossiping with friends, or window-shopping. By all means, en-

joy these pastimes, but only in moderation and *after* you've done more important things. Take a look at how you spend your "down time." Could you accomplish other activities during this time? Activities that would assist you in attaining your goals? Your important goals must come first; pastimes come afterward, if time is available.

Another technique is to set aside time periods each week for specific activities: Monday, 9:15 to 10:00, dictate correspondence; 10:00 to 11:00, make rounds of selling floor; and so on. During very important time periods, have calls held and allow no interruptions. This will ensure that your important activities get done first. Many successful people even block off time for exercise, hobbies, and other pastimes to make sure they don't spend excessive amounts of time on these enjoyable activities. Whatever technique you use, be certain you make effective use of nearly every minute you have available.

Avoid Busywork

Are you busy all the time, but unable to get a great deal accomplished? Perhaps what's keeping you busy has little or no relation to the important goals you need to accomplish. Take a look at what you spend your time on and ask yourself if you really need to do all those things to attain your goals. If not, discard the activity or spend less time on it.

Does reading all your mail carefully help you in your goals? What about reading articles, journals, and reports? Could you quickly scan these materials? How much time do you spend making small talk with friends? Do you attend unnecessary meetings? Do you spend time filing, keeping records, or doing other clerical duties your secretary could perform? Your activities should lead to important accomplishments; you should not spend time on busywork. Attaining goals leads to success, but busywork only leads to being busy.

Delegate Responsibilities

One of the most effective ways to manage time is to delegate as many tasks as possible to those who work for you. These extra responsibilities will keep your employees highly motivated and fulfilled in their jobs. In addition, you'll be free to take on really productive tasks. Which activities could you delegate? List these tasks and then choose the person best qualified to do each one. Explain each job carefully when you delegate it, and be sure that your people know they can come to you if they need help in doing it.

To delegate extensively requires trust and confidence in those who work for you. If you do not believe in your employees' abilities to get the job done, you will want to do it all yourself. But that is a wasteful, unproductive way to operate. It is much more productive to let others take on as much as they can. If you don't trust your subordinates, ask yourself why. If you doubt their skills and abilities, then coach and counsel them until you're sure they can do the job. If they show no improvement over time, you may have to take more drastic action. But if skills, abilities, and motivation are there, your lack of trust is probably due to you and not them. Show more confidence in the staff and delegate as much as you can. You may be surprised at how much they can do.

Hire Others

Many people feel pressed for time because they try to do everything themselves instead of hiring additional people. This is particularly true of entrepreneurs developing their own business. For example, if you run an income tax service by yourself, there is a practical limit on how many returns you can do, no matter how many hours you work each week. You'd get more done and earn more money if you hired someone to assist you.

Hire part-time help first, and then get full-time assistance as your business expands. You cannot be a leader of others if you do everything yourself. Nearly every type of success requires an eventual transition into management of others. So take that step and use your time more effectively.

Similarly, if you work for a business or industry, you may need to add staff to take on additional tasks. Present your case to your superiors. Use facts and figures to show that you need additional staff. Show how these new people will improve quantity of work, quality, efficiency, or response time. If you present your case effectively, you may very well get the extra workers you need to do the job properly.

Time is valuable and irreplaceable. Don't squander it on unimportant activities. Use your time and that of others as efficiently as possible.

PARTICIPATIVE MANAGEMENT

Never make a decision yourself, if you don't have to.
—Henry Doherty

Participative management has been around for a number of years and enjoys a spirited revival from time to time. Briefly stated, participative management is a technique that relies on delegating matters to the lowest possible level. When job-related decisions must be made to improve quality, lower costs, reduce scrap, or improve the quality of work life, employees who actually perform the jobs in question determine the best way to proceed. The boss retains veto power for solutions that are impractical or too costly. This contrasts with the authoritative style of management in which one person makes all decisions and others have no say in the decision-making process.

Many techniques—including quality circles and participation teams—employ the participative management concept, but these are "the sizzle, not the steak." While these techniques allow employees to work as a group to solve problems, the approach will not work unless management is willing to use the employees' ideas. True participative management is a consistent style that always involves employees in decision-making and problem-solving; it is not effective if it's done only in connection with certain programs such as quality circles. Truly participative management requires a substantial effort, certainly more than just setting up quality circles.

Many leaders fear that participative management is no management at all, that if employees make decisions by themselves, there will be no need for managers. Nothing is further from the truth. Under participative management, the boss is still the boss and has final decision-making authority, retaining veto power on all decisions. Instead of making all decisions independently, however, the boss allows employees to suggest solutions to some problems and then implements their solutions in many cases. The participative style is nothing more than thorough delegation, where appropriate. That is not a loss of power, but a wise use of human resources.

To gain more insight into participative versus authoritative management, let's consider an example. A manager in a service company is faced with a problem. Everyone in his unit goes out to lunch at the same time, leaving no one in the office to answer the phones. As a result, important calls are not being received, costing the company potential customers. Now, let's see how two different managers handle this problem.

Arthur E. Tative draws up a schedule, requiring each of his five clerical employees to cover the phones one day each week. He tells the employees that they must eat a brown-bag lunch on the day they are assigned to cover the phones. To avoid paying overtime, Arthur allows the employee to go home an hour early on phone-answering day.

Arthur feels confident he has come up with the right solution; it will not cost the company money, and he will have phone coverage every day. Arthur calls the employees into his office, announces his decision, and gives everyone a copy of the schedule. He says they will start the new process next week.

After three weeks Arthur is happy. The phones are covered, and he is getting his messages. However, Linda Q. tells Arthur that she does not like having to cover on Fridays all the time. Since Friday is payday, Linda likes to go to the bank during the lunch hour. She cannot do this now, and by the time she leaves work in the evening, the lines are long at the bank, which makes her late in getting home.

Debby B. also is unhappy with the schedule. She tells Arthur that she likes hot lunches, but now is forced to eat cold sandwiches on Tuesdays, her day to cover the phones. In addition, she has had indigestion every Tuesday because it is impossible to eat lunch and answer the phones at the same time. That makes her nervous, and she has to eat hurriedly. And employees in other departments don't have to cover phones during lunch hour, so why should she?

Arthur is perplexed. He thought the problem through very carefully, came up with an equitable and fair plan, and yet people are unhappy. Arthur concludes that he did a good job with his plan, but that it is impossible to make everyone happy. No matter how hard you try, some people are going to complain. That is just the way they are. He decides to leave the schedule the way it is. If people complain any more, he will take disciplinary action.

Del E. Gate, the second manager, is faced with the same problem. He calls his five employees into his office and explains the problem and how it affects his department. He asks his employees to work out a solution on their own. Del says he'll listen to what they come up with, but will retain veto power if the solution is impractical. If, for example, the employees suggest hiring a temporary employee just for the noon hour or installing an expensive answering system, he will not accept their recommendations. But if they develop something practical, he will implement it. The employees are to report back in a week with their solution.

One week later the employees present their solution to Del. Each employee will cover on a different day of the week, Nancy on Monday, Joan on Tuesday, and so forth. On the day they answer the phones during the noon hour, they will take an early or late lunch hour at their discretion. In addition, they will rotate the days each week. If Nancy has Monday this week, she will have Tuesday next week, Wednesday the week after, and so on. Also, they can trade days to answer the phones in any week if both parties choose to do so.

All employees are content with the solution and proud of the work they did to create it. Del thanks them for their work, says he likes the plan, and it will start next week. Del feels it is a good plan, won't cost the company anything, and will ensure that the phones are answered.

After three weeks everything is running smoothly for Del. He is receiving his messages, and the employees seem content with the process now that they're used to it. Del is proud of his employees' solution and admits he might not have come up with as good a plan himself. The plan works, and the employees are content.

Both Arthur E. Tative and Del E. Gate reached the same goal: they set up a system for receiving phone messages during the noon lunch hour so that they would get their messages. However, their means of doing so were entirely different. Del was very participative in obtaining the solution. His employees are happy with the system. It tested their abilities, and they enjoyed that. They were closer to the problem than he was and had their own ideas to offer. Since it was *their* plan and not *his*, they accepted it very readily.

Arthur, on the other hand, was very authoritative. His approach brought dissatisfaction. He dictated to the employees, and, as a result, he has a morale problem. His employees think the plan is unfair, and they had no say in the decision whatsoever. Arthur's employees will do as they're told, but they'll resist the plan in subtle ways. This could cause absenteeism, low productivity, and terminations unless they can convince him that there is a better way.

In these two examples it should be clear that the participative approach of Del E. Gate did not lead to a loss of control. He had veto power, and he could have suggested alternatives if necessary. Instead of using his own time to come up with a schedule, Del was able to concentrate on more important problems while his employees did the scheduling task. His technique permitted a better use of his time. But he is still very much the boss and in control of others.

By implementing participative management techniques you can delegate some problems to your staff without losing your control, and you can get the results you want at a savings in your own time. We sometimes associate leading with barking out orders, but leading often consists of giving direction and letting others come up with the solution to a problem. Allow your employees to use their brains to the fullest extent in improving productivity and the quality of the work place. That will be more satisfying for them and for the company as well.

IN PRAISE OF PRAISE

> *He who praises everybody praises nobody.*
> —Samuel Johnson

Countless studies have shown the effectiveness of positive reinforcement in getting people to do what you want them to do (see B. F. Skinner, *Science and Human Behavior,* or *Contingencies of Reinforcement*). Positive reinforcement means providing things of value to someone when you get the behavior you want, and withholding such rewards when you do not get what you want. For example, if you get the detailed technical report you want, you praise the employee who wrote it. If you get consistently high performance from certain employees, you promote them or give them a significant salary increase. The praise, promotion, and money are all the positive reinforcers for the behavior you desired.

For positive reinforcement to be effective, it must be clearly linked to the desired behavior. Too often in business or industry, the link is nonexistent or far removed from the behavior. You establish this link by your behavior and what you say. For example, you might say, "I am promoting you because of your exceptional achievements over the past two years and the skills you have." Or "I am giving you this salary increase because your work exceeded the job requirements during the past year." That link between the reward and the good performance will sustain the desirable behavior. People will continue to do what you want because by doing so they obtain the rewards they value.

With no reinforcement, the good performance is likely to cease. Employees will think, "Why should I work harder when I never get anything for it?" It is very important for you, as the leader, to establish and maintain the link between job behavior and rewards. Interpret the work environment for your employees and show them what they can attain by doing certain tasks. Otherwise, they may not see the relationship. Remember that there are many forms of positive reinforcement other than material rewards. Praise and status, for example, are controlled by leaders who can distribute these rewards as they see fit. They do not cost anything, so make wise use of them.

Of course, there is also negative reinforcement: punishment, the "slap on the hand" for poor performance. There is a big difference between negative reinforcement and no reinforcement. No reinforcement means simply withholding rewards when an employee fails to achieve; negative reinforcement means a verbal warning, discipline, or termination when the employee fails to achieve.

Many studies have shown that positive reinforcement is clearly more effective in bringing about improved job performance. So, if you want your employees to do their best work, use rewards. Although negative reinforcement can make employees aware of their problems, it is less effective in bringing about improved performance.

At times, of course, you'll have to use negative reinforcement. If an employee walks off with $25,000 of the company's money, you must, of course, deal with that swiftly and negatively. You cannot afford to take time to develop the person's honesty through positive reinforcement. Immediate negative reinforcement is needed. And so it is with any other serious conduct violation.

When it comes to developing new skills, taking on more work, or correcting minor performance problems, however, you can help your employees become more effective by taking a positive approach. Over the long term, your people will see that good performance always leads to a reward, so they will always strive for superior performance.

Positive reinforcement works because people enjoy getting whatever they value. If you like praise and receive praise for doing a good job, you will try to do a good job in the future to get more praise. If you value money and know you'll get a large bonus for exceptional performance, you will perform exceptionally to get more money. Obviously people value different things. Some may want praise; others want money, promotions, growth, learning, or more responsibility. But they will work to attain more of whatever it is that they want. You, as their leader, must provide those rewards and explain how they're linked to performance.

Positive reinforcement also has an indirect effect on employee performance. If you compliment someone on a job well done, the person values that compliment in itself. However, the compliment also has the indirect effect of boosting the person's confidence. The employee will think, "I know I'm on the right track if the boss thinks I did a good job. I am going to try even harder the next time."

This will sustain good performance over time. The positive reinforcement (in this instance, the compliment) begins a cycle: praise leads the employee to try harder, which leads to improved performance, which leads to more praise, and so on, endlessly. As this cycle repeats itself, your people gain confidence in themselves and begin to believe they can do even better—and as a result, they will do even better.

In this way, you gradually shape your employees' behavior by giving reinforcement for successful completion of each task on their way to a distant goal. For example, let's say you have an employee whose ultimate goal is to produce one hundred widgets a day. You can reward this employee as he reaches various milestones on the way to this goal. When he produces fifty widgets a day, praise him in front of everybody. When he reaches seventy-five, post the news on the bulletin board. This shaping process reinforces your employee's confidence, tells him he's on the right track, and encourages him to proceed further. If you withhold all rewards until this worker reaches a hundred widgets, he might quit trying before he gets close to his goal. But the shaping—giving rewards along the way—is likely to result in continued striving toward the goal.

There is evidence, however that reinforcement works best when given occasionally rather than after every single successful accomplishment. Suppose you have a new typist who's trying to cut down on the number of errors she makes. If you praise her after every error-free letter, memo, or report, you'll create a problem. Your praise will lose its value, and if you forget to praise just once, the employee may think you no longer care. As a result, she may stop trying to improve further.

Instead of constant compliments, provide praise once a week or so. The employee will then be likely to persist, unconcerned about lack of praise after each letter. Infrequent praise is more effective than frequent praise, but all praise must be linked to performance and given out only if earned.

Positive or negative reinforcement is one means by which employees come to understand what kind of workers they are. If you tell people they are incompetent and worthless, they will believe you and act that way. If you tell them they are skilled and hardworking, they will behave accordingly. You, as a supervisor, control the employees' perception of their ability.

Although positive reinforcers are usually in the form of praise, money, and promotions, there are other, more subtle means of reinforcing good behavior. Say an employee approaches you with a new idea. She wants to convert the records system in the department into a computerized system. You say it won't work and it would cost too much, without even hearing her out. What have you done? You've provided negative reinforcement; you've told the employee not to suggest new ideas. If the employee never comes to you again with a new idea, you have only yourself to blame, not her.

Suppose that, instead of dismissing the new idea, you give it your full attention and thank the employee for taking the initiative. You provide positive reinforcement, regardless of whether you later implement the suggestion. Employees will come forward with more ideas in the future if they know you reward suggestions with your attention and consideration. Listening attentively is a subtle form of reward, but it can help you get the most out of your employees.

6•

Creativity: Another Key to Success

THE NEW FROM THE OLD

> *We must assume that there is probably a better way to do almost everything.*
> —Donald M. Nelson

> *I do not believe you can do today's job with yesterday's methods and be in business tomorrow.*
> —Nelson Jackson

Creating something new—something that many people need or want—can be the beginning of a long, successful career. But, you say, I'm no Thomas Edison. I don't have that kind of creative genius. I can't make something out of nothing.

Stop and think for a minute. Look around you at the most recently created products—microwave ovens, for example, video recorders, computer games. Did their creators make something out of nothing? Or did they take an existing product and modify it in such a way as to produce a different kind of product? That's what most creativity is—the ability to combine several existing ideas into one "new" idea, or several existing devices into one "new" device.

Take a product like the digital watch or the pocket calculator. The digital readout system for these products was developed by NASA for use in space flights long before pocket calculators and digital watches were available. Then all it took was for someone to see that this readout system could be modified slightly, mass-produced, and marketed to the public. And that is exactly what happened. Digital watches and pocket calculators did not have to be developed from scratch, but only modified from something that already existed. But someone had to have the vision to see how space technology could be used in commercial products for the consumer.

You do this kind of creative adaptation all the time. You pick up an idea from someone, or read some interesting facts, combine that with some other existing information, and you come up with something new. You have created without even knowing it.

You might read an article about the increasing life span, and that gives you an idea about a new product or service for senior citizens. Or you notice that the people in your community travel quite a distance to visit a popular restaurant, health club, or store, and this gives you the idea to open another outlet nearby.

Thousands of existing ideas, facts, products, and services are sitting around waiting for you to adapt them into something new. The need for creative change is constant. What worked well ten years ago will not necessarily work well today. Many highly successful people have the ability to anticipate future needs and come up with creative ways to capitalize on those needs. Highly successful real estate people will anticipate what the public will be looking for next year, and then prepare to meet those new needs before their competition does. New car designers, to be successful, must anticipate what the public wants and come up with models to meet the future demand.

How do you anticipate the future? In three ways. First, you do research. You read surveys, articles, and newspapers. Then you correlate all your information—by relating oil prices and oil shortages to the need for smaller cars, for example. And third, you respect your own gut feelings. Your hunches, remember, arise out of the skills, abilities, and knowledge you have in your field. Your own competence will tell you the direction in which things are headed. Do your research, correlate your information, and then take your gut feelings into consideration as you strive to anticipate future trends.

While you are increasing your own creativity, you can also begin to surround yourself with creative people (see Chapter 10). Constantly encourage your employees to come up with new ideas. Praise them when they do so, and implement the ideas when you know they will contribute to the company's success — and therefore your own.

Above all, keep your mind open to new ideas. Never believe, even for a moment, that things are perfect just the way they are now. This attitude commonly leads to stagnation and failure. In contrast, continuous creative change brings with it needed improvements and very often leads to success. It also produces some anxieties, of course. It takes courage to discard the old and design and implement the new, but change is crucial to success. Creative, successful individuals say things like this:

- "Let's try to do it another way."
- "I have an idea on how we can improve this."
- "Let's revise our procedures for handling that."
- "We need a new system for the department."
- "I would like to improve the quality in our area."

These attitudes lead to more effective performance. Ask yourself some questions about your own creativity. How do you react to new ideas and to change? Are you receptive to these ideas, or do you complain about them? Do you initiate improvements without being asked? List the improvements you have initiated in the past six months. Could you do more? Do you present your ideas for changing things to others or do you keep them to yourself? Unless you take them to others, the ideas are of no value to anyone.

You can do several things to increase your creativity. Here are some suggestions.

Brainstorm

Think of ways to revise, improve, or vary the products your company produces. Come up with ways to improve the methods, procedures, and systems you are responsible for. For example, can you reduce the cost of clerical assistance by storing information in and generating reports from a computer? Can you save fuel by installing a computer-controlled thermostat system? Can you increase sales by offering a free workshop for potential clients?

List as many ideas as you can, recognizing that you cannot pursue all of them. You are interested in coming up with alternatives, not critically evaluating each one. Schedule a brainstorming session periodically; it will eventually become a regular part of your thinking.

Seek Ideas from Others

Ask others how things can be improved. Get suggestions from subordinates, superiors, and peers. Combine their ideas with your own to come up with the best composite. Implement the creative ideas of others in addition to your own.

Use Information Resources

Read books, journals, and newsletters in your field. As you read, ask how you can use this information. Will this, or some variation of it, work for you? If you learn that other firms are using job-sharing, ask what it could do for you. In some cases the direct application to your setting may not be immediately obvious, but keep an open mind anyway. Be willing at least to play around with the idea. Many times, you'll see how you can benefit from applying other companies' ideas.

Search for Links

Try to find new connections between various facts, events, data, and information. If you read that unemployment is going up, ask what this means for your company and what you can do about it. Are interest rates going up? How does that relate to your own capital expenditure plans? Tie in the new information with the old and think of all possible results.

Analyze Problems

Analyze your main problems and ask yourself and others what is causing them. List as many causes as you can. If the rejection rate on one of your products is too high, your list of possible causes might include faulty raw materials, poor equipment, or unskilled staff. Pinpoint the most likely source of the problem by gathering more information. When you have identified the source, come up with creative ways to eliminate the causes of the problem.

PERSPECTIVES ON PERSPECTIVES

A New York lawyer who wanted to buy a summer home found just the right one on a small island off the Maine coast. Approaching an old man painting a boat, he inquired about the owner.
"Place belongs to the Hallet boys," the man said, and pointed to a dot in the distance. "That is Ben Hallet over there. Out haulin' his lobster traps—he'll be in in a couple of hours. Ben's the smartest feller around here. Seen him dig eight, ten bushel of clams in one tide. Gits good money for 'em too."
"And the brother?" inquired the would-be buyer.
"Waal, he ain't near so smart as Ben. Didn't amount to much—lawyer or sumpin', down in Boston."

I can complain because rose bushes have thorns or rejoice because thorn bushes have roses. It's all how you look at it.
—J. Kenfield Morley

You can greatly enhance your creativity by learning to look at existing viewpoints from a different perspective—if you can flip ideas over and see them from a different angle. A change in perspective will give you a new awareness of alternative approaches that may be more successful than your current approach.

Here's an example of the value of changing perspective. A human resource management consultant specialized in helping companies set up selection systems, management development programs, and career guidance programs. He would develop programs and then turn them over to the client company. At one point his consulting business began to dry up.

The consultant advertised more, made more personal contacts, and sent out flyers, but to no avail. The business simply was not there. A downturn in the economy had led companies to postpone or curtail the type of programs he offered.

The consultant thought of ways to beef up business. Since increased advertising did not help, he next thought about offering companies programs in different areas. But he concluded that companies would see these new programs as low-priority items. He continued to think about creative solutions to the problem. One day he picked up a copy of a career guidance kit he had developed for a client company and later sold to a second firm.

He came up with the idea of marketing the career guidance kit to individuals, not just to companies. With unemployment on the rise, the idea seemed perfect for individuals. The kit could be sold directly to people who were looking for jobs and switching careers. He advertised these kits in newspapers and magazines and wound up selling thousands.

Those career guidance kits had been right under the consultant's nose every day. Yet he had not thought about selling them to individuals. He had to change his perspective only a slight degree to find a solution to his problem.

And so it could be with you. The solution to a work problem may be sitting on your desk waiting for you to notice it, or it may be lurking in the back of your mind somewhere. If you're consistently seeing poor quality in a certain product, for instance, you may be looking in the wrong place for the cause and the solution. You've been searching for something that your employees are doing wrong, perhaps, but you haven't been able to put your finger on anything. All right, then, look somewhere else. Are the raw materials of a poorer quality lately, maybe? Are the screws that hold the products together a fraction of a millimeter too long or too short? Turn the problem around and around until you find the solution.

You can do other things to change your perspective. Don't limit yourself to your own perspectives. Take advantage of the ideas others may have. Also, when you talk to someone whose viewpoints are different from yours, try to identify with those other viewpoints. If you combine them with your own opinions, a new composite might emerge that is better than what you started with.

Another technique you can use is to turn to that role model you used earlier. Ask yourself what this person would do about a certain situation. This can help you see things from a new perspective. The more perspectives you can consider, the greater the chance you have of coming up with a creative solution to maximize success.

7·

The Art of Learning

NEVER TOO SMART

Half of being smart is knowing what you're dumb at.

Many receive advice, few profit by it.
—Publilius Syrus

The most successful people never stop learning. They have a continual need to know more. They seek out fresh information and combine that with their previous knowledge to come up with something new. New information becomes available every day. Many people say, "I can't learn all that." The highly successful simply open the book and start reading.

Since the world does not stand still, you must constantly learn more or you will find yourself out of touch and out of date very quickly. Acquiring knowledge in your field of expertise is critical for success, so it is important for you to consider what specific subjects you need to learn about. Draw up an inventory of what you know right now. That will help you determine where you need to gain additional knowledge. To begin this process, list the specific knowledge and skills you need in your current job. Be as detailed as you can. List all of the subjects you must understand in order to do your job well. Be very specific here. If you are involved in labor relations, for example, don't put just "labor relations" on your list; write down every facet of the subject you must understand: grievance procedures, contract negotiation techniques, and so forth.

Your next step is to evaluate your knowledge of each subject on your inventory list. Use a rating system of some sort; score yourself on a scale of 0 percent to 100 percent, for example, or A to F, or 1 to 10. This step, if you are honest with yourself, will help you see where you need to increase your knowledge.

When you've completed your evaluation, you must set yourself some goals: "Take a course in labor law," for example, or "Read two books about negotiation techniques." Then set out methodically to learn more about each area in which your knowledge is weak.

ARE THERE ANY QUESTIONS?

> *Curiosity is one of the most permanent and certain characteristics of a vigorous intellect.*
> —Samuel Johnson

> *No man really becomes a fool until he stops asking questions.*
> —Charles P. Steinmetz

Learning results from asking questions. It makes no difference if you ask these questions of someone else or pose the question to yourself, as long as you obtain the answer. Never worry about appearing stupid when you ask a question. Curiosity, remember, is a mark of intelligence. How many times have you heard people say, "That's a good question," or "I'm glad you asked that." Always keep in mind that people *like* to be asked questions; it shows that others regard them as experts.

It is the person who never asks questions who appears to be

stupid. By asking questions and getting the right answers, you can learn something you might otherwise never know. Some kinds of information simply will not come your way unless you ask.

Most successful people have the confidence to ask questions when they want to know something. At meetings, they ask questions until they have all the answers they need. In their offices, they reach for the phone, dial a number, and ask one question after another. If the president of the company can ask questions, why can't you? If you postpone asking questions and tell yourself you're waiting for exactly the right time, you'll cheat yourself, because the right time may never come.

You should not be intimidated in asking questions. If someone calls you asking for information, you don't assume the person is dumb. On the contrary, you probably regard the caller as smart for seeking out more information and having an inquisitive mind. People will perceive you the same way—as an inquisitive person trying to learn more. That is a favorable reputation to have. So approach questioning without fear, be assertive, and go forward with confidence.

Asking questions goes beyond merely seeking people out to get more information. Whenever a report crosses your desk, review it with an open yet skeptical mind. Be willing to learn from the material and use the information, but continually ask yourself questions such as these:

- "How can this be improved?"
- "Was anything left out?"
- "What conclusions can I draw from this?"

These are constructive questions. They indicate that you take the report seriously and intend to act on it. Get the answers to all your questions by seeking out the person who wrote the report. By asking questions about that report, you'll learn a great deal, and others will perceive you as an interested, concerned employee. That perception can help you in your quest for success.

Never let yourself believe that you know all the answers to everything, or that asking questions is beneath your dignity. That is a very foolish attitude to take. It shows that you have a closed mind on a subject, that you have no wish to learn, and that you have little potential.

Remember that inquisitiveness is one key to success. Continually probe for the answers you need. Never be afraid to ask. If you feel intimidated in some situations, ask questions anyway. Force yourself to be assertive and press on. Asking questions will mark you as someone who is trying to make improvements by getting to the bottom of things.

LIGHTNING BOLTS

> *The thoughts that come often unsought, and, as it were, drop into the mind, are commonly the most valuable of any we have.*
> —John Locke

> *All thought is a feat of association: having what's in front of you bring up something in your mind that you almost didn't know you knew.*
> —Robert Frost

Much knowledge comes from external information sources—people, books, television, newspapers, or computer data banks. But learning can also come from within. You can, from information already in your brain, derive new ideas and in this way learn from yourself.

These ideas often strike you suddenly, like lightning bolts. Learn to take them seriously, for they are often an excellent means of solving problems and deriving new knowledge. The ability to take advantage of lightning bolts varies greatly from person to person. As you might guess, highly successful people appear to take advantage of spontaneous ideas more often than less successful people.

Have you ever tried to solve a difficult problem at the office, been unable to come up with the right solution, and then, while relaxing at home, had the perfect solution come to you? Why did the solution come to you when you were not trying to solve the problem? Part of the explanation is that you were under pressure to get a lot done at the office, and perhaps you were also constantly bombarded with phone calls, visits, and memos. Pressure and interruptions always make it difficult to concentrate.

When you're at home, however, or relaxing in a restaurant or park, you can let your mind wander a bit; the immediate attention required by the job is gone. That's why solutions to difficult problems may suddenly become crystal clear.

The subconscious part of your brain may have been working on the solution to a problem all day. All you need is an opportunity for the subconscious solution to drift into consciousness. Then, suddenly, the right answer simply appears. Such ideas may be lost forever if you don't relax now and then. Set aside some time each day—early in the morning, late at night, after lunch, or whenever you will not be disturbed or distracted—and let your mind travel anywhere it wants to go. Find a spot where you can be alone, preferably out of reach of doorbells and telephones. Put out of your mind all thoughts that require concentration or provoke anxiety. Make yourself as relaxed and comfortable as possible.

Your free thinking can have some direction, if you wish. You can steer your mind to areas related to your work or even to specific problems. But don't try to force a solution by deep concentration. You tried that earlier in the day, and it didn't work. Instead, let your mind wander from one idea to another until it comes up with some possible answers. You can evaluate these ideas in detail later; for now merely generate ideas.

Your free ideas may even stray from the main topic. If so, go ahead and let your mind wander. More serious concerns in your subconscious may deserve more immediate attention than the problem you started with. You'll be surprised how effectively you can solve problems if you just let your ideas flow. Don't blot out any ideas; let them all come forth. The right answer is there someplace.

While doing this unstructured thinking, keep a notepad and pencil handy so you can jot down ideas that come to you. Some good ideas may come to you in the middle of the night or at other times when you least expect them. You might keep a notepad at your bedside and carry one in your pocket or purse wherever you go.

Another way to increase your ability to come up with solutions is to repeat the problem to yourself over and over. Say, for example, "I need to find a way to cut overhead by ten percent." If you can't take time to discover the solution while you're saying this, let your brain do the work while you go on to other things. If you put this idea into the subconscious part of your mind, ideas may pop up when you are relaxed and not trying to come up with the solution.

If you are one of those people who never think about business while at home, you will not benefit from this technique. You must be willing to think about business problems even during your leisure time; that is extremely important for your success. In summary, to cultivate spontaneous ideas, do the following:

- Set aside a time for free, unstructured thinking.
- When new ideas come into your mind, seize them.
- Enhance purposeful free thinking by physically and mentally relaxing in a private, quiet area where you will not be disturbed.
- Keep your thinking loosely structured, but guide your mind in certain directions if you wish.
- Keep a notepad at your bedside and in your purse or pocket wherever you go. Write down all of the ideas you come up with.

If you can put these suggestions into practice, you will be a step ahead of those who allow themselves no time for free thinking. Remember that many, many great ideas have come to successful people when they were not trying to come up with the idea.

AN OPEN MIND

According to the theory of aerodynamics, as may be
readily demonstrated through wind tunnel experiments, the
bumblebee is unable to fly. This is because the size, weight and
shape of its body in relation to the total wingspread
make flying impossible.
But the bumblebee, being ignorant of these scientific truths, goes
ahead and flies anyway—and makes a little honey every day.
—Sign in a General Motors plant

Man's mind stretched by a new idea never goes back
to its original dimensions.
—Oliver Wendell Holmes

Look at new ideas with an open mind. By giving these ideas thoughtful consideration, you can learn, improve on existing practices, and achieve better results. A closed mind guarantees that your world will stay the same; no improvements will be made. Change is often vital to success, so consider all new ideas carefully, even if they seem at first to be radical departures from the norm.

Some people wholeheartedly resist change, perhaps because they feel they already know the best ways to handle a given situation. Change therefore represents a blow to their pride, as if they are being personally criticized for the way they do things. Also, change can provoke anxiety, for it may force people to abandon long-standing patterns and strike out into new, uncharted territory. That makes some people feel extremely anxious, regardless of whether the change is just a new idea they are asked to think about, a new way of managing they have to try, or a move to a new city. The fear of change is often worse than the change itself. Afterwards, most people say, "That wasn't so bad after all."

Highly successful people do not close their minds to new ideas. They implement those ideas that will help them attain their goals, and they discard the bad ideas after careful consideration. They look at change with an open mind; they see it as crucial to remaining in front of the pack. Let's look at two production managers, only one of whom keeps an open mind.

Doug Matic is a line operations manager in a medium-sized industrial plant. He has been in his current job for five years and has been with the company twenty years altogether. Doug Matic's counterpart at another division is O. Ben Mind. Ben, like Doug, has been with the company for over twenty years and has been in his current job for three years. His line operations authority is comparable to Doug's.

Doug Matic and O. Ben Mind have both been called into a meeting with their boss, Hy Upp, who is general manager for manufacturing operations with the company.

"I appreciate both of you stopping by this afternoon," Hy says. "I asked you here to kick around an idea. As you know, we need to improve production. I've been talking to some of our competitors, and they've all started programs in participative management. These programs involve teams from the bargaining unit and management who get together to discuss production and the quality of work life. The teams generate suggestions for improvement, and the good ideas are acted upon.

"Our competitors furnished me with some information on the success of these teams," Hy continues as he distributes some reports. "The teams have come up with ideas worth a few hundred thousand dollars over the past year at one company. The others have had similar results. In addition, absenteeism and grievances are down at one company, though no definite results are available for the others. While it costs money to hire a consultant and train people in team techniques, our competitors feel this is the way to go. I think this technique might work for us, but I'm not absolutely certain. That's why I've asked you here. What do you think? Should we consider participative management?"

"That will never work here," Doug Matic declares. "Our people will never participate in this. The average employee here just wants to get the job done and go home. They don't want this team stuff. They'll consider it a waste of time."

"I'm not so sure about that," O. Ben Mind replies. "The average worker here today wants to do more than just perform routine tasks. These workers want to use their brains as well as their brawn."

To that, Doug retorts, "Listen, I've been here twenty years, and I know how to manage this place. The supervisors and I will make any changes we need. Why do we need to ask the bargaining unit how to do it? We didn't hire them for that."

"They're closer to the work than we are," Ben says, "and we have a lot of other things to do. If they come up with good ideas, why not use them? I already do that whenever I can, but a formal program like this would help me."

"I don't feel we need to change," Doug insists. "We've been in business for seventy years and earned a profit every year but three. Why change things?"

"Because our profits haven't been good," Ben says, "and this new system might help. I don't think it's a cure-all, but it could raise our profits."

"How do you think your supervisors will respond to this?" Hy asks them. "Would they support it?"

"They'll hate it," says Doug. "There's no way my supervisors will buy into this. They'll say it's crazy and resist it."

"I think my people would give it a good shot," Ben says. "They might be a little uneasy at first, but they'll try it."

At this point, Hy ends the meeting. "I'd like the two of you to go back to your supervisors and see what they think. Let's meet again a week from today and decide if we should pursue this any further."

Now, let's pick up the scene later in Doug Matic's office. Doug has pulled his supervisors together and given them an overview of Hy's request. He now continues: "Well, that's all I know about it. It'll never work here. Hy got these reports from our competitors. You can take a look at them if you want, but I'm not going to read them because I know this process is a waste of time."

Supervisor No. 1 says, "But some of our employees like to come up with ideas. This program could be good for them. And we might improve productivity."

"I'm not sure it'll work," says a second supervisor. "The start-up costs could be high, and maybe people would expect too much."

Supervisor No. 3 says, "When I was in the bargaining unit I might have been suspicious of this, but I would have tried it. If it'll make you feel more responsible and important to the company, you'll give it a try."

"There's no way you'll convince me that we can set up these teams," Doug insists. "There are just too many reasons against it. The workers don't want it. My mind is made up."

Later at O. Ben Mind's office. Ben has given his supervisors an overview of Hy's request, and then he continues: "I've read these reports, and the results are really impressive. Here are copies for each of you. Well, what do you think? Is this something worthwhile for us to think about?"

Supervisor No. 1 likes the idea. "I think we should try it. People have ideas that could help us. We need to improve quality to remain competitive. Maybe this is the way to do it."

"Yeah, that's true," says Supervisor No. 2. "I don't think this program will hurt, but I'm a little skeptical. Still, we need all the help we can get from everyone who works here."

Supervisor No. 3 adds, "I think the idea is good. Maybe we could pilot test the teams in just one section rather than all over the place at once. That way we could see if it works without involving too many people. Then we could expand it to include other groups."

"I think that's a good idea," Ben remarks. "Let's learn from a small cross-section and go on from there. I'll report back to Hy that we'd like to give it a go on a small scale first."

Doug Matic clearly was not receptive to the ideas Hy was suggesting. His mind was made up from the very beginning, and he never tried to view the situation openly. He refused to read the information Hy provided and did not really listen to his supervisors. Ben, on the other hand, was willing to look at the situation with an open mind. He listened to Hy, responded to Doug's comments, and picked up on his staff's idea of pilot testing the program. His approach was flexible and indicated a willingness to learn and adapt.

Who is to say whether the team approach will work for this company? It might, and it might not. The important point is that one manager was willing to look at the situation with an open mind and one was not. If the idea *does* work, it could mean many thousands of dollars in savings for the company.

But you have to have an open mind on the subject to attain those benefits. If the thinking pattern of the two managers persists over time, the open-minded manager will pass by the other manager because of his willingness to make improvements. Some of the new ideas will work, and that will enable him to attain better results.

Now analyze your reactions to new ideas. Think back to the last few times your boss, a peer, or subordinate suggested a novel way of doing things. Did you approach the idea openly or resist it? What did you say when you first heard the idea? Were your comments of the open-minded or close-minded type? In general, are you like Doug Matic or O. Ben Mind? Do you take suggestions from others? Has a closed mind ever prevented you from considering an improved way of doing things?

You can do a number of things to make yourself more open-minded:

- Consider all new ideas seriously. Instead of hastily concluding that something will or will not work, be willing to play around with the idea. You can always discard it later, but never do so immediately.
- Be willing to try out those ideas you are uncertain of. Give them a shot and see what happens. Objectively evaluate the idea's effectiveness on the basis of actual results. Then decide if the idea is worthwhile or not. If it's not, you can return to the old way of doing things.
- Recognize that change will make you anxious, but remind yourself that you will feel much better than before because you will be more effective.
- Force yourself to adapt to necessary changes. If you hold on to the old ways, you will never grow and develop. And that will likely lead to failure.

An open mind is vital in your quest for success. It will help you select the best idea from all possible alternatives. Remember that change is essential if you wish to remain ahead of the rest. Be willing to look at other people's ideas with an open mind, and also aggressively seek out as many new ideas as possible. Obtain the ideas of other experts, your staff, superiors, and anyone else whose opinion you respect.

8·
Knowledge

KNOW NO KNOWLEDGE?

> *To the small part of ignorance that we arrange and*
> *classify we give the name knowledge.*
> —Ambrose Bierce

> *Strange how much you've got to know before you*
> *know how little you know.*

We are all in the knowledge business. No matter what line of work you are in or what personal goals you have for yourself, knowledge will be an important factor in your success. A well-known Arab proverb is useful for classifying people with respect to knowledge.

There are four kinds of people with respect to knowledge:

The person who doesn't know and doesn't know that he doesn't know: he is a fool, forget him.

The person who doesn't know and knows that he doesn't know: he is a student, teach him.

The person who knows but doesn't know that he knows: he is asleep, light a fire under him.

The person who knows and knows that he knows: he is wise, follow him.

Most people fall into one of those four groups; successful individuals are usually those who know and know that they know.

It might be helpful to translate that proverb into a business setting to see how people fall into the different categories. You are an invisible observer at a meeting in a large insurance company. A claims manager, Clem D. Nide, has asked his four supervisors to attend a meeting in his office.

Clem D. Nide: It's one-forty. I'd like to get started, but I wanted Hope to be here as well. Does anyone know where she is?

Hope Less (entering the room): Gee, I'm sorry I'm late, but I could have sworn your secretary said the meeting was in the conference room.

Clem: Now that we are all here, let's get started. I've asked you all here because of a problem we are having. Our payment level for health care claims has escalated dramatically for the months of November and December. We're up something like eighty percent over normal for the past two months. Yet, at the same time, our premiums are dropping off. Because of a downturn in the economy, unemployment has escalated. And those unemployed typically don't carry health insurance, resulting in a loss in premiums. My boss wants to know what's going on and what will happen in the future. And I'd like to have your thoughts on the subject.

Hope: I think it's a shame that claim payments are going up.

Emma Wise: My data show that the high payment level peaked right around the first of the year. Our payment level for the first half of January is only five percent above normal. We should be back to normal levels very soon.

Clem: But what's the reason for the high payments in November and December?

Emma: December is always a high month for us. Because of the holidays and vacations, people are likely to schedule lab tests and X-rays. In addition, the deductibles on claims must be paid for all services provided after January first. People can avoid the deductible by having the work done before the first of the year. So that's why our claims payments are higher at the end of the year.

Hope: I had an X-ray taken in December. It was negative.

Stu Dent: I'm still not real familiar with our payment process yet, but what Emma said seems plausible to me. Isn't it possible some of those unemployed will continue their health care coverage for a few months after they're laid off? And perhaps schedule elective surgery during that time?

Clem: That sounds reasonable. Noah, you haven't said anything yet. How do you feel about all of this?

Noah Moxie: I can't really be sure, but my opinion—and it's just my opinion—is that the payment level has peaked. In fact, according to my projections, we will actually be seven to ten percent below normal for the first quarter of the year. I agree with the reasons given so far, but I might add that studies have shown that when economic conditions worsen, stress levels increase, and this causes health care usage to increase as well.

Emma: Yes, that's true.

Stu: And, isn't it possible that such people might stock up on prescription drugs, knowing that they may not be reimbursed for such prescriptions once their health insurance expires?

Emma: Right again. We have evidence of that.

Hope: That reminds me. I need to refill one of my prescriptions.

Clem: Noah, do you have evidence similar to Emma's?

Noah: Well, it's still tentative information, and we aren't absolutely sure, but I believe that those unemployed show a forty percent increase in health-related problems after layoff. Also, and this is also tentative, there is a thirty percent increase in prescription use the month before health insurance expires. We need to verify this, though.

Clem: I want to thank all of you for your thoughts on the subject. You've been very helpful. I have a much better understanding of where we are now and where we are going.

If you supervised these four individuals, you would handle their development differently. Emma is in command of the situation right now. She needs a promotion or new assignment to keep her from becoming bored with her job. Give Emma as many different and challenging assignments as you can and move her on to higher-level responsibilities.

Noah has the abilities, but needs more confidence. Assertiveness training would help him. Also, reward Noah for speaking out and taking charge. Developmental assignments could include a task force or committee where Noah is forced to come out of his shell, lead a group, and show what he can do.

An employee like Stu needs more knowledge and experience to perform at a higher level. He could benefit from the experience of someone like Emma. Give him a thorough orientation, and expose him to as many aspects of the work area as possible. Seminars and workshops could also benefit Stu, as could participation in task forces where he could learn from the rest of the group.

If you have someone like Hope working for you, good luck. The best development you could provide her with is to deal with her lack of knowledge as frankly as you can. If she's had sufficient time on the job and shows no improvement, you must consider giving her another assignment or even terminating her. Merely letting her continue to babble will not do anyone any good.

Which one of the four categories do you fall into? Do you know your area of expertise well and let others see your knowledge? If so, that makes you similar to most successful people. Or do you know your area well, but feel unsure about expressing yourself? In this case, build confidence in yourself by recognizing your competence. Speak out more. Act like the expert you really are. Or perhaps you are still learning some new functional area. If so, you must continue to build on your existing knowledge base.

GENIUSES AND FOOLS

> *Fools need advice most, but only wise men are the*
> *better for it.*
> —Benjamin Franklin

> *A learned fool is more foolish than an ignorant fool.*
> —Molière

> *Let us be thankful for the fools. But for them the rest*
> *of us could not succeed.*
> —Mark Twain

Extremely successful people are regarded as geniuses in their fields. Exceptionally high intelligence is believed to be the reason for their success. But is there any truth to this belief? Is being a genius essential to attaining great success? Studies have shown that intelligence does have a modest correlation with success, at least where success is measured in terms of promotional advancement or job performance (see John P. Campbell, *Managerial Behavior, Performance and Effectiveness*). People with higher intelligence levels have advanced further or performed better than those with lower intelligence levels. However, many other traits mark the most successful people. Intelligence appears to enhance success, but it alone will not lead to success. You must have other skills going for you as well.

The available research (Lewis Terman, *The Gifted Group at Mid-Life*) suggests that being smart is very helpful in attaining success, but that being a genius may or may not produce additional success. The smart individual has enough intelligence to grasp and process relatively complex information, learn from it, and develop new ideas. This is essential to be a successful leader in business. Average intelligence is required to perform many jobs, and intelligence beyond the average level is usually an asset. However, extremely high intelligence is an asset only if you can put it to use in your job.

An extremely intelligent person may not find administrative

responsibilities all that challenging, and might prefer instead to work on solving highly complex problems or creating new products or services rather than drawing up next year's budget or reviewing and approving expense statements. In fact, the extreme intelligence of a genius might actually interfere with success in many jobs, since that person might well be frustrated.

Isaac Newton, Albert Einstein, and several other famous scientists are regarded as geniuses. But others with extremely high intelligence have not been successful at all and have held odd jobs or been unemployed. Why is this? Perhaps it happens because many jobs do not take advantage of such intelligence. Another reason is that success depends on other traits in addition to intelligence. You need to have many other things going for you, and you must be in the right career to take advantage of your knowledge.

Higher intelligence will assist you in your career, but it is a mistake to think you will never attain great success because you are not a genius. That simply is not true. Many successful people are not geniuses or even intellectuals. They have other characteristics that enable them to attain success. Extreme intelligence, by itself, will guarantee you nothing but a high score on an IQ test.

Look now at some factors that determine how high intelligence can be effectively put to use:

Ability to Apply

Someone could have a tremendously powerful intellect and yet be unable to apply that intellect effectively. For example, a person may have the intelligence to figure out the cure for cancer. But to find the cure the person must be able to gather the necessary information, test ideas, write up results, and communicate those results to others. That takes time and many skills. If these activities are not done, that intellect goes to waste, and the problem goes unsolved. It is the same in any other field of endeavor. You may have the intelligence to accomplish tremendous goals, but unless you can apply yourself, nothing will ever happen.

Motivation
If you are exceptionally intelligent, but not motivated to put your intelligence to use, then you accomplish nothing. Success depends upon both intelligence and motivation; either one alone will not lead to attaining goals.

Perseverance
Without perseverance, intelligence will go to waste. Many people have excellent ideas, but lack the determination to follow them up. Someone with a great deal of perseverance will forge ahead until he or she reaches a goal. To get any mileage out of high intelligence, you must persevere.

Creativity
What is described as genius is often just a combination of ability, creativity, and drive. The ability to create is independent of pure intellectual ability. You can be extremely creative and not be particularly intelligent, or be extremely intelligent but have little creativity. Put intelligence and creativity together with a strong desire to achieve and you will probably be a success. Without creativity, intelligence is useful only for understanding and learning complicated things, not for developing new, innovative concepts.

Information Seeking
You can effectively put your intelligence to use by aggressively seeking out all the information you need and then doing something with it. Ask questions, and aggressively seek out written information. Then put it all to good use.

Effective Management
To use intelligence effectively, you must be capable of managing yourself and possibly others. Managing includes making efficient use of time, setting goals, and prioritizing tasks so

intellectual capabilities are concentrated on the most important areas. In addition, you must manage your resources effectively, whether those resources are human, mechanical, or financial, so as to give yourself time for productive thinking and for using your intellectual capabilities.

Having a great mind will help you achieve success, but you also need all these other skills and characteristics. Ask yourself if you are putting your intelligence to the best possible use. Can you apply your intelligence? Are you motivated? Do you persevere? Are you creative? Do you seek out more information? Can you manage effectively? If your answer to any of these questions is no, you must try to improve in that area to get the fullest use out of your intellectual capabilities.

Remember that you must keep on learning year after year. If your reading is limited to mystery novels, seek out diverse nonfiction books, magazines, and journals. You can learn a great deal from these. Watch educational television programs. Take courses. Pursue studies on your own. You can even play games that will help you build your vocabulary or your math skills. From all of these activities you will learn and, more important, you will learn how to learn, which is what intelligence is all about.

9•

Effective Communication

THE SPOKEN AND WRITTEN WORD

Conversation in a store:
"Do you have any four-volt two-watt bulbs?"
"For what?" asked the clerk.
"No, two."
"Two what?"
"Yes."
"No."

A young employee wrote the following advertisement
for a new kind of soap: "The alkaline element and fats in this product
are blended in such a way as to secure the highest quality of
saponification, along with a specific gravity that keeps it on top of the
water, relieving the bather of the trouble and annoyance of fishing
around for it at the bottom of the tub during his ablutions."
A more experienced writer later wrote the same thing in two words:
"It floats."

Our exceptional ability to communicate with other human be-
ings distinguishes us from other species. We spend much of our
lives communicating with others, and it would be impossible
to lead a normal life without communication in one form or
another.

We communicate in three ways: speaking, writing, and body language. Speaking and writing are the clearest ways to communicate, but body language—facial expressions, posture, and gestures—also conveys a great deal about what you are feeling. At times, in fact, nonverbal body language may tell more about what someone feels than the person's words.

Being an effective communicator will help you succeed in attaining the goals you have set for yourself. You don't have to become a polished public speaker—many successful people are not—nor do you have to be a professional writer. However, research has shown a correlation between effective communication and overall success. Good communicators attain more than ineffective communicators. Think of some highly successful people and compare them to highly *un*successful people. Which ones communicate better?

For those employed in business or industry, communication skill has a direct impact on success, since this skill is likely to be included on company performance appraisals. Good communicators will receive high appraisal ratings, and a number of rewards usually go with those higher ratings.

Moreover, communicating effectively will enable you to accomplish important company goals and in this way hasten your promotional advancement. High achievers get promoted quickly, and their communications skill is one reason for their achievements.

Let's discuss some ways to improve your communications skills.

Be Brief

When you speak to a group or to an individual, be succinct and stick to the point. Provide all information your audience needs, but omit unnecessary details. You've had to listen to long-winded speakers drone on and on, and you want to avoid falling into that category yourself. Don't risk boring your audience. Say what you have to say and then be quiet.

The same holds true of written communication. Keep your reports and memos brief and to the point. People have a limited amount of time to read. Provide short, capsule summaries along with detailed reports so that people can read the summary before deciding whether to read all or part of the detailed report. In this way, you can communicate effectively yet avoid burdening others with tons of paper.

Know Your Audience
Tailor your messages for the intended recipients. If you are an engineer and need to describe a new technical device to your fellow engineers, you can explain the technical detail of the device. However, if you must describe the same device to a group of nontechnical executives, provide a general overview rather than technical information. If your audience consists of people in the community who have no detailed insights about your company, limit yourself to very general descriptive information about what the technical device does. Put yourself in their shoes and ask, "What would I like to know about it?"

Speak Plain English
Some people believe that their readers or listeners will be impressed if they use long technical words. Actually, it works just the opposite way. Those who write or speak too technically are perceived as out of touch, too academic, or too technical. That reputation will hurt your career, not help it. If you find it difficult to choose between unfamiliar words and familiar ones, err on the side of the familiar.

Trendy terms and buzzwords put people off. If you are talking to people who are likely to be unfamiliar with the jargon of your trade, then don't use it.

Be Clear
Carefully choose the correct words to convey your message. You will have more time to be precise with written than with oral communications, so go back and reread memos or reports to ensure you have said exactly what you meant to say. Rewrite the material until it says exactly what you want it to. With oral communication you will not have that second chance, so choose your words carefully.

Use Body Language Effectively
The use of effective body language greatly enhances an oral message. Gestures, facial expressions, and posture all convey a message to the recipient. That message must agree with the verbal message. If you say, "I'm not angry," make sure you don't clench your fists as you speak. Such a conflict between verbal and nonverbal messages will leave the listener confused and perhaps disbelieving. Be conscious of the nonverbal messages you send, and make sure they coincide with your verbal messages. Excellent books on body language include Desmond Morris, *Manwatching*, and Julius Fast, *Body Language*.

Evaluate your communications skills, including speaking, writing, and body language. If you need to improve in any area, you can do so through independent study, formal courses, and communications training. Practice also helps greatly.

I HEAR YOU

> *Most of the successful people I've known are ones who do more listening than talking. If you choose your company carefully, it's worth listening to what they have to say. You don't have to blow out the other fellow's light to let your own shine.*
> —Bernard Baruch

> *Remember what Simonides said—that he never repented that he had held his tongue, but often repented that he had spoken.*
> —Plutarch

Skill at listening is every bit as important in communicating with others as are speaking and writing. Have you ever talked with someone who didn't listen to you? That's not a conversation because no message gets communicated. Effective listening is an important component of any conversation.

Listening means giving thoughtful attention to what the

speaker says. Reflect, concentrate, and make certain you've got the message straight. Make comments about what the speaker has said. Or make a mental or written note of it.

Highly successful people are very careful listeners. They comprehend the speaker's message very quickly, make a judgment about it, and respond appropriately. They know that listening is an important means of becoming successful, and that by listening they can learn what someone else knows. Successful people, in their quest for knowledge, are more interested in learning and listening than in saying things they already know. The new information may help them reach new goals, improve on existing methods, or acquire new skills, thus leading to further success.

Another aspect of listening involves reading the body language and facial expressions of the speaker. These nonverbal forms of communication indicate the speaker's emotions. If you can effectively interpret the verbal and nonverbal together, then you will likely be a very effective listener. Build proficiency in both components through individual study and through practice.

Good and bad listening can be illustrated by a scene involving two managers, Al Talk and Alice Enner, each of whom supervises a number of employees in a service organization. Joe, an employee in their department, goes to them with a personal problem. Here is how the two managers respond.

Al Talk: Joe, what is it you wanted to see me about?
Joe: Well, Mr. Talk, you see, I've been having a problem. I—
Al: What's the matter? Personal problems again? Look, Joe you're just like everyone else in this company. So what if you have a problem? You've got a job to do, and you can't let things bother you.
Joe: Well, I know, but I need to talk to someone—
Al: Now listen to me. There's nothing wrong with you. I have problems, too, you know. Just yesterday my kid smashed the fender on the car. Cost me four hundred dollars to get it fixed. Can you imagine that? Boy, was I mad! But I don't let it bother me one bit at the office. No, sir, I've got a job to do here, and I do it. Nothing bothers me.

Joe: I know that, but, you see, I can't control this problem I have, and I'm worried about it.

Al: Joe, the best thing you can do is to stop worrying. It never gets anybody anything. Forget about your problems. Go out and have a few drinks.

Joe: That's just it, I—

Al: Listen, Joe, I'd really like to help, but I've got a lot of work to do. Now you get back to your job and stop worrying. I'll see you later. Okay? Thanks for stopping by.

Now see how Alice Enner handles the same situation.

Alice Enner: Joe, I understand you wanted to talk to me. What's on your mind?

Joe: Well, Ms. Enner, you see, I've been having a problem. I ... I ...

Alice: Go ahead, tell me what your problem is. I'll try to help if I can.

Joe: Well, I started drinking after my divorce, and I'm worried about it. It hasn't affected my work yet, but I'm afraid of what's happening.

Alice: Have you been drinking while on the job?

Joe: No, just before and after work.

Alice: How much have you been drinking?

Joe: I don't even know. I've been losing track of things a lot lately.

Alice: Well, it sounds to me as if you have a serious problem. I'd like you to see a counselor about it. The company has a program that can help you.

Joe: Gee, that's just what I was hoping for. I sure need to talk to someone about this and get help.

Alice: I'd like you to call Dr. Bill Jones at this number. I'll tell him to expect your call. Can I count on you to do this?

Joe: You sure can. I just want some help and to get better again.

Al Talk and Alice Enner responded very differently to Joe's problem. Al did not listen at all to Joe. He didn't even let Joe finish most of his sentences. As a result, Joe never even had a chance to explain what his problem was. And because of this, he got no help at all. Al heard Joe, but he didn't listen.

Alice Enner took a very different approach. She listened to Joe and responded to the things he had to say. She offered advice only when it seemed appropriate. She made Joe feel at ease and encouraged him to express himself. That is thoughtful, effective listening. Because of this, Joe was able to get help with his problem. Effective listening gets better results.

Review your listening skills. Do you give thoughtful attention to others? Do you react to what they say? Or do you insist on doing all the talking? Do you assume the role of a listener at least some of the time? Do you pay attention to the facial expressions and body posture of the speaker? Do you allow others to express their feelings? Do you try to get people to open up and speak their thoughts if they seem reluctant to do so at first?

How can you improve your listening skills? First, make sure you are not doing all the talking. Sit back and listen much of the time. Concentrate on what the speaker has to say and pay attention to facial expressions and other nonverbal signs. Also force yourself to repeat mentally what the listener has just said or summarize the speaker's thoughts out loud. If you review what was said in this way, you are likely to retain the information much better, and this will enable you to practice effective listening skills. When listening, ask yourself questions like, "Why did he or she say that? What does this person's body language tell me?" That will help you understand more than just the words. Help in acquiring listening skills is available through books and even special workshops. Seek out assistance if needed, and do whatever else you can to master this important communication skill.

COMPLAIN, COMPLAIN, COMPLAIN

Remember, when you are telling people your troubles, that half of them aren't interested and the other half are glad you're finally getting what's coming to you.

You may talk of all subjects save one, namely, your maladies.
— Ralph Waldo Emerson

Complaining is an activity in which many people heartily participate, though they would do better to avoid it. When you are working toward success, certain frustrations are bound to occur. Your boss may make a decision that goes against your better judgment, resources may be too scarce to get a job done, you may fail to get that big promotion, or your performance rating may be lower than you had hoped. There are many ways to react to such frustrations, and one way is to complain.

For some people, complaining becomes a way of life. Even when they are not particularly upset about something, they seize every opportunity to complain and criticize. Being a constant complainer is incompatible with being a success. When others hear you complain frequently they will think, "Why should I do my job when we have these problems at our company?" Complaining is negative and derogatory because it draws attention to what is bad rather than what is good. Successful people focus on the good.

Complaining is also contagious. If one person starts complaining, others are likely to join in. After a while you can have an entire department or company griping. As a result, the work climate will be negative. That is why it is so critical for you as a leader to emphasize the positive and discourage widespread complaining. If an employee is unhappy about something, take that person aside and discuss the problem. Don't let him or her ventilate hostility on co-workers.

As a leader, you must ensure that complaining is absolutely minimal in your work unit. Keep your own complaints to yourself or discuss them in private with your boss if necessary. Don't set a bad example by complaining openly yourself, and don't allow others to do so.

To see how complaining affects others, look at this scene in an administrative department that has been short of clerical staff.

Moe Gripes: I tried my best, but the boss won't add any more people. He said we'll just have to get along with what we have. I can't understand this company and the way they operate. It was never this way at the other company I worked for. We always had plenty of clerical staff there. But here, it's always different. Our managers never listen to us here. They just don't understand the problems we have. That wasn't the way the managers were at the other company I worked for. They always listened to you there.

Staff Member No. 1: Well, what should we do now?

Moe: Just do what you can. If you can't get all the work done, don't worry about it. Maybe the boss will listen to us if the work piles up to the ceiling. This place is crazy. Just yesterday Joe told me that some employees are thinking about starting a union. You can't blame them at a place like this.

Staff Member No. 2: Do you think we should join a union?

Moe: No, I didn't say that. I only said you can't blame people for thinking that way. I mean, with all the troubles at this place, it's no wonder people are thinking that way. I bet we lose more good people than most other companies do. But that's just the way it is here. This place is sure different than the other place I worked at.

Now see how another manager handles the same situation.

P. Ray Zem: I asked my boss about staff increases, but the company just can't afford to add anyone right now. We'll have to manage better with the resources we have. Can we manage things differently to save clerical staff? I want to do a first-class job, but we need some other options. What ideas do you have?

Staff Member No. 1: One thing we could do is get a word processor. I probably spend half my time retyping memos and reports that could be done in a few seconds with a word processor. That would probably save two hours every day that I could use for other activities.

Staff Member No. 2: We also have to do some unnecessary forms and paperwork. They could be streamlined and put up on the computer. That would save a lot of manual filing and checking, maybe two hours a day.

Ray: Those are great ideas. We already have word processors in the company. I'm all for streamlining forms and paperwork, too. Let's think through how to do that right away. As for computer storage, we already have the terminal here. I'll call Jim Johnson in Systems to see if he can come over and work out the storage and retrieval of our department's information. If we implement these suggestions, will we be able to get everything done without the staff addition?

Staff Member No. 2: We should be able to.

Ray: Well, that's great! I'm glad we had this discussion. Let's get to work on implementing the results right away. Thanks for your help.

Moe Gripes and P. Ray Zem took different approaches to the same problem. Moe complained about the company, its management, and the decision not to add staff. He also tossed in some gripes about possible unionization and turnover and even encouraged his staff to do poor work. If you worked for Moe, how inspired would you feel? Would you try hard to do your best? Or would you think about quitting and going to work for someone else?

Ray, on the other hand, got his staff to come up with time-saving ideas to improve productivity. His approach leaves employees feeling good about the company and their jobs. As a result, Ray's department will likely have better productivity and higher morale.

Moe Gripes, of course, is an extreme type of complainer, but even more subtle forms of complaining can have a detrimental effect on others. Take stock of your own behavior with regard to complaining. Do you take swipes at your company, your boss, or peers? Do you criticize the decisions reached by management in your company? Do you complain about the shortage of staff, lack of money in the budget, or changes in priorities?

How about personal problems? Do you bore others with your financial problems, you bad back, or your troublesome children? If so, you give out this message to others: "I am a loser. I am unhappy. I can't handle my problems." That is not the message you want to send out if you are hoping to obtain success. And your staff will not follow you if they think you are a loser and complainer.

At times everyone experiences frustration and wants to ventilate those feelings to others. The best approach is to avoid doing this openly. Tell the specifics to your boss in private or talk to a counselor or a friend away from work, if you wish. But do not complain at work. If you are upset with a lack of funding for that pet project of yours, instead of complaining, ask your staff for ideas about getting it done more cheaply or without funding. If you miss out on the promotion you hoped for, do not complain to everyone and set yourself up as a loser. Instead, ask your boss what you can do to get promoted.

Some people will introduce a positive suggestion by expressing a complaint. For example, you might say to your staff, "I don't like this. How can we make it better?" Or you might say, "The company is having problems with such and such. What can we do to improve matters?" In this way the complaint serves to introduce a positive request, so it is acceptable. A better alternative, however, is to mention the positive request without the negative lead-in. Simply say, "How can we make it better?"

SELLING YOURSELF

Unless the man who works in an office is able to "sell" himself and his ideas, unless he has the power to convince others of the soundness of his convictions, he can never achieve his goal. He may have the best ideas in the world, he may have plans which would revolutionize entire industries. But unless he can persuade others that his ideas are good, he will never get the chance to put them into effect. Stripped of non-essentials, all business activity is a sales battle. And everyone in business must be a salesman.
—Robert E. M. Coure

The ability to sell is important in attaining success. Selling a product is, of course, vital to the success of many people, but there are other equally important kinds of selling. Consultants, lawyers, and physicians, for example, sell their services. Creative people sell their ideas. Artists sell their talents. And when you seek a new job or a promotion, you have to sell yourself. Also, you may have to sell an idea to someone; maybe you want to sell your employees on the idea that they should work harder, or sell yourself on the belief that you'll profit from doing something you really don't want to do.

In any of these endeavors, the best salesperson usually comes out on top. The consultant who is most effective in explaining what he or she can do for you will probably get the contract. The job seekers who convince you that they are qualified will get jobs. The more effective you are at selling, therefore, the more successful you will be in attaining your goals. You can do a number of things to sell effectively. Follow this sequence of steps when you conduct a sale:

Assess the Client's Needs

Start by finding out how your product or idea will benefit your client. Place yourself in the client's shoes. Visualize the sale from the client's point of view. What kinds of needs do you have? What sorts of questions would you ask the salesperson?

In one column list the client's needs. Then determine how your product, service, or idea will fill those needs. Write this information in a second column. If the client wants to save money, for example, write down the ways your product will help. If the client wants to save time, show how you can save time.

If what you have to offer does not meet the client's needs, think of other products, services, or ideas you can make available. But be certain that you offer something that will make things better for the client, not just for yourself. It is the client who must be happy with what you have to sell.

Plan Your Presentation

Use the information from step one to come up with a step-by-step presentation for the client. Direct this presentation toward meeting the client's needs. Think through the whole presentation. What will you say and do? How will you respond to questions? You may want to use facts, figures, transparencies, or other visual aids to drive home your key points. Visualize yourself conducting this sales presentation successfully. Rehearse the presentation several times.

Seek Out Your Client

Set up a time to meet with the client. This may mean calling and saying you would like a meeting, or it can entail aggressively seeking the person out and devising a way to get some time with the individual. Regardless of how this is done, make the sales presentation the single item on the agenda. Avoid making your pitch as merely one item out of many to be covered in the meeting. That will dilute the effectiveness of the sale. Simply tell the individual what you would like to talk about. A long lead-in will make your client anxious and resistant. This meeting can take place in an office, at a restaurant, or on a golf course. Use your best judgment as to the setting.

Present Your Case Objectively

In making a sale, the objective approach usually works best. Show the client how you can meet his or her needs. Break away from your plan only to answer questions the client asks during the presentation. Be positive and upbeat. Emphasize the good that will come from buying what you have to sell.

Try to Gain a Commitment

During the sales presentation, gain some kind of commitment from the client if possible. For example, if you are trying to sell the boss on giving you the afternoon off, you can get an immediate commitment during the sales presentation. If you are selling yourself as a job candidate, of course, do not seek an immediate response. Final decisions in some cases will take time and thought and involve other people. If you pressure your client, the person may become anxious. However, you can get an agreement that the idea is a good one and a promise that the decision-maker will give it additional thought. Seek this form of commitment with some deadline set for a final decision.

Conduct a Follow-Up

Many sales are lost because the person doing the selling gives up after the initial presentation. You may need to talk with the client again and provide additional information even if it is not requested. To assist along these lines, set up a tickler file containing notes and specific dates on which to check on the progress of the sale. Persist with your follow-ups until you get the sale. In many cases a no will later turn into a yes.

To see how these steps work, imagine that you are the manager of a training department for a large company. Your department has done some impressive work that has received national attention. As a result, you would like to offer training program assistance to any company willing to pay for the service. This consulting service will still be a part of your parent company, and profits earned will go to the company. Individual bonuses would be paid to consultants, in addition to a salary, depending on the success of the consulting venture. You think this is an excellent service for your company to offer, but must sell your boss on the idea. Here is how you plan the sale:

Step 1—Assess the Client's Needs

The clients in this case are the people who must approve the start-up of this consulting venture within your company—the company president and your boss, who is the vice-president of personnel. Both individuals have similar needs, and therefore you can plan your approach to both in much the same way. You identify the following needs for both individuals:

1. Need to offset the costs of personnel operations with some form of profit.
2. Desire to have a nationally recognized personnel function.
3. Need to have new management development programs without incurring extra costs.

You decide that setting up a consulting service group within the training department will fill these needs. The consulting service will generate income from the sale of its training programs. It can also develop new programs for other companies for a fee, which will fill needs number one and three. As a result of the marketing and sale of these training programs, the company's personnel function will become widely known, thus filling need number two.

Step 2—Plan Your Presentation

You do some homework and find out that about $20,000 worth of initial marketing should generate in excess of $100,000 in sales of existing training materials. Costs will also be incurred for reproducing videotapes and manuals ($8,000), postage ($1,000), and staff support ($15,000). The total costs, including marketing, are $44,000, leaving a profit of $56,000. You place this information on a flip chart to present to your boss. These figures are very conservative, but you do not want to oversell the approach.

You will offer to track staff time on all consulting activities separately to ensure bottom-line results. The consulting group will be run as an independent cost center and must turn a profit to stay in business. To address the need for new management development programs, your game plan includes the provision that marketing will seek out clients who desire these programs. Company employees would work on the project part-time with their salaries offset by the client's fees. Once the program is developed, it can be used within the parent company at no cost.

You incorporate all the information into a step-by-step presentation. Charts and handouts reflect the results to be obtained through this consulting service. You rehearse the presentation several times until you are confident that you can convince your boss of this new program's merits.

Step 3—Seek Out Your Client
This step is easy: you merely set up a meeting with your boss. You reserve enough time for a comprehensive presentation and ensure that no other items are on the agenda. You tell your boss what you want to discuss so there will be no surprises.

Step 4—Present Your Case Objectively
You present your material in a well-organized, objective way and show your enthusiasm for the idea. You have anticipated most of your boss's questions and have appropriate answers.

Step 5—Try to Gain a Commitment
You know that your boss cannot make the final decision to approve this venture. That must come from the president. However, you ask for his assurance that he will give the venture additional thought. Your boss agrees to do this. You request an opportunity to present your case to the president, and your boss agrees to consider this.

Step 6—Conduct a Follow-Up

Two weeks after your presentation, you call your boss and ask about the consulting service. Perhaps he'll tell you he has been talking to others in marketing and public affairs about it, and he'll try to set up a meeting with the president.

To get others to buy what you have to sell, use the steps outlined here. Be assertive, seek people out, and let them know what you have to offer. Go to the decision-makers. Success always involves selling something, so master this important skill.

10•
Promotions, Staffing, and Development

THE RACE TO THE TOP

If you wish in this world to advance,
Your merits you're bound to enhance;
You must stir it and stump it,
And blow your own trumpet,
Or trust me you haven't a chance.
—W. S. Gilbert

Plenty of men can do good work for a spurt and with
immediate promotion in mind, but for promotion you want a man in
whom good work has become a habit.
—Henry L. Doherty

Most employees want to be promoted into higher-level jobs. However, there is a great difference between having the *desire* to be promoted, having the *potential* to be promoted, and actually getting the promotion. And getting that promotion is what separates the winners from the losers.

Some companies spend a great deal of time and effort identifying people who are on the fast track and expected to advance. Yet, in the long run, many of these high-potential people fail to advance for a variety of reasons. Potential, by itself, will get you nowhere.

Realizing your potential is something else. If you work as hard as you need to, achieve all that you are capable of achieving, and pursue your goals methodically and relentlessly, you will realize your potential. Then, chances are, you'll be promoted.

By putting into practice the suggestions offered in this book, you'll help to ensure that promotion occurs. Let's review some of those key suggestions in the context of promotional advancement and add several new suggestions.

Convince Others You Are the Best

Obtaining a promotion often requires convincing someone you are the best person for the job. You cannot promote yourself, and so you must persuade someone else to do it. To accomplish this you need to seek out the key decision-maker, explain that you want to advance, and then show that you're the right person for the job. Do your homework: determine the requirements (knowledge, skills, experience) for the position you aspire to. Then show the decision-maker how you meet or exceed those requirements and convince the person that it would be a mistake to not promote you.

It makes no difference if the job you want is vacant or not. Set yourself up as the successor for the time when the position becomes vacant. In fact, it makes no difference if the job currently doesn't exist. If you see the need, you can create a new position that combines the responsibilities of existing jobs or adds entirely new responsibilities. Present the reasons for establishing this new job. Be objective, but show how the position would benefit the company. You might very well attain that new position as a result of your efforts.

Regardless of the type of position you want, try to obtain some sort of commitment from the decision-maker. You will not get an immediate agreement to promote you, so don't seek one. Instead, gain commitment from the decision-maker to consider your qualifications further and to think about you when a higher-level position becomes available. Continue to remind this person occasionally that you are eager to be promoted and that you're the best one for the job.

Set Yourself Apart

If you want a particular promotion, make sure you stand out from your peers. You can distinguish yourself in many different ways. You might be more knowledgeable, work harder, be a better manager, or be more results oriented. But unless you stand out, you will not be seen as any different from the other candidates, and you will not likely be chosen. To set yourself apart, you need to understand your strengths and weaknesses and the requirements of the job you want. You also want to know your competition for that job. Orient your approach to show why you are a better choice than the others. Do not assume that the decision-maker will deduce this independently. Take the initiative to sell yourself. But do this positively by emphasizing your strengths, never by denigrating others.

Be Reliable

To get promoted you need experience, education, knowledge, skills, and abilities. But you also need to be reliable. The boss must know that he or she can count on you to get the job done. Establish yourself as someone who can be counted on to come through. Your reliability will be inferred mainly from your current job performance. If you consistently get results, that will certainly stand in your favor. Reliability is the mark of the winner, someone who is capable of performing at a higher level.

A reliable person comes through day in and day out, even under great pressure or with limited staff and resources. This person is reliable all the time, not just when a higher-level job is vacant. Bosses can very easily spot the person who suddenly becomes a star when a job is vacant and then goes back to a lower performance level. Steady reliability plays an important part in the decision to promote.

Character

Character often enters into promotional decisions. Those making such decisions will look beyond job performance to see if the individual has integrity. Traits such as trustworthiness and integrity become increasingly important as you ascend the corporate ladder, given the sensitive nature of most high-level positions. The potential manager must have a strong code of ethics if he or she is independently to run a large unit of the company. If you lack integrity, the promotion you want will go to someone else.

Strong character and integrity must be evident in your work standards. A manager must set the proper tone for others through high standards and hard work, and personal example sets that tone best. If you demand a high-quality product, refuse to tolerate poor work, and expect honesty and integrity of others, your character will come to the attention of key decision-makers. Also, if you work long hours, do not waste time, and are oriented toward bottom-line results, that too will be noticed. Decision-makers know your standards will become those of your staff. Ensure that you are perceived as favorably as possible with regard to work standards.

Commitment to the Company

Before promoting you to a higher-level job, your superiors will undoubtedly discuss and evaluate your commitment to the company. Try to make sure that they know from observation certain things that convince them you are very committed indeed to the organization. Here are some things they should have noticed:

- You are willing to spend extra hours at work in order to get the job done right.
- You'll willingly put forth any amount of extra effort that is needed to complete a task properly and on time.
- When necessary, you will make personal sacrifices for the sake of getting the results the company wants and needs.
- You have consistently supported company policy, you show no signs of becoming a rebel, and you never criticize or complain about company policy.
- You have made it clear that you regard your employment at this company as permanent.

Let's take a closer look at that last observation. Your bosses won't promote you, you know, if they hear that you're always on the lookout for a better job at another firm. What would be the good of promoting you if you're likely to turn around and resign three months later? Any job-hunting you do will have to be so subtle as to go completely unnoticed by your managers.

Patience

Surveys of the top executive officers of major corporations have shown that the vast majority have worked for only one or two companies in their entire careers. They advanced through the ranks to get to their current positions; they were not hired from the outside. That suggests that, in most circumstances, staying with your current employers is a more likely road to success than hopping around from one firm to another.

Most companies like to promote from within to take advantage of their current employees' knowledge of the company and also to save outside recruitment costs. Outsiders have a particularly difficult time entering higher-level positions since they lack familiarity with the firm. That puts them at a disadvantage in comparison to current employees at the company.

In certain circumstances, however, you'd do best to consider changing companies. If you can get a whopping promotion—say, two or more job levels above your current position—the switch may be beneficial. But be careful not to take a job similar to your current one but with a more impressive job title and a few thousand dollars a year more. Look at the responsibilities, span of control, staff size, and budget authority to determine if the new job is a significant promotion. If it is, the big increase in pay will offset the loss of accumulated pension and vacation benefits at your current company. If the job is a lateral move or involves only slightly greater responsibility, you will lose on the move even with a salary increase.

It's also appropriate to make a switch if your company is in poor financial shape or declining in size. In such cases, a move to a growing, financially healthy company could benefit you, even if the new job involves the same kinds of responsibilities. The move could offer you long-range promotional opportunities and, eventually, higher pay and better benefits.

Do your homework and think carefully about switching from

one company to another, however. You don't want to trade one set of problems for another, and you can't afford to be regarded as a job hopper. Only if the move offers greatly increased responsibility or movement away from a failing company will a switch be in your best interests.

A few final comments are in order about promotional advancement. Although most people are interested in promotions, nearly everyone will stop advancing at some point. Not everyone becomes chairman of the board. "Pyramid effects" ensure fewer and fewer positions at successively higher levels in the company. And the vast majority of managers will stop moving ahead at some level lower than that of chairman. The level at which you stop advancing will depend on your abilities and on how well you develop yourself.

For some, the end of advancement is a source of frustration, and so they jump ship and head for another company. Often, such a move is unwise. The person may be no better off than before the move. In those instances it would have been better for the person to work on improving performance while continuing in the same job. Promotions are important and you should aspire to them, but be honest with yourself and keep your expectations realistic.

SQUARE PEGS IN SQUARE HOLES

When you hire people who are smarter than you are,
you prove you are smarter than they are.
—R. H. Grant

A lad once asked Mozart how to write a symphony.
"You're a very young man," Mozart told him.
"Why not begin with ballads?"
"But you composed symphonies when you were ten years old,"
the youth pointed out.
"Yes," replied Mozart, "but I didn't have to ask how."

To attain great success, you must have excellent people behind you. Regardless of what area you choose to succeed in, you cannot do all the work by yourself. It makes little difference how hard you work or how long you work; you must count on others to help you achieve your goals.

A successful enterprise is a lot like a baseball team. Unless it has the right players in the various positions, the team will not do well. Even one poor player can result in a loss for the entire team. It is the same way in business or industry. Your work team must be composed of excellent people in all positions or you will not win the game of sales and profits against your competitors.

As you build your staff, you must insist on getting the best possible person for the job. The extra productivity of exceptional performers has a tremendous dollar impact on the company, and an exceptional performer may do the work of two or more less talented people, saving additional staffing costs. So, as you review prospective job candidates, do not be content with average people who just meet the job requirements. Keep searching until you find an exceptional person, even if others tell you that such people do not exist.

Don't rush to fill a job vacancy, even if you feel a need to get someone on board quickly. Putting an average person there quickly could cost you thousands of dollars in decreased productivity over the years. It is better to leave the job vacant a few weeks or even months until you find the superstar you want.

It is critical for companies to have extremely competent people in the highest positions. People tend to hire those who are similar to them, so if the top people are superstars, they will probably hire exceptional performers. That can start a cycle that will lead to a very successful enterprise. But if a company tolerates less effective people at top levels or allows others to do so at lower levels, then less success will result. Outstanding companies should have a firm policy of hiring only the best. They should practice this in their recruitment efforts and be willing to pay a premium for exceptional people. It will pay off in good results.

Some managers fear having highly competent people behind them. This fear is based on the suspicion that a highly competent subordinate may outperform the boss, be after the boss's job, or make others realize that the boss is not indispensable after all. Such suspicions, which reflect the manager's insecurity, can cost the company a great deal of money, for the manager who feels this way is almost sure to hire mediocre people. You must not fall into this trap. Keep in mind that having highly competent people behind you is to your advantage. A department or function staffed with competent people will enjoy the respect and confidence of everyone else in the company.

Never fear superstar employees who do an excellent job and take on more assignments than anyone else. Encourage such people by giving them more responsibility and letting them take on more important tasks. Top managers want and expect you to have good people behind you, people who can take your place when you move up. In fact, your own promotion could be delayed, or even denied, for lack of a suitable successor. So hire the best people you can find, for the sake of your own career as much as for the success of your company.

If you make an effort to hire the best, how can you be sure of getting the best? Here are some steps you can take in hiring staff members.

Define Your Needs
You must know what you are looking for before you can go out and get it, so a good starting point is to analyze the job you need to fill. Examine the job and list the experience, education, knowledge, skills, and abilities required. List the important job qualifications and determine the level of performance you expect. Stick to objective, measurable, clearly definable characteristics. Use this information when screening resumes and when interviewing job candidates. An example is as follows:

Position:	**Manager, Public Affairs**
Experience	10–15 years in public affairs or public relations, at least 3 years in a managerial capacity
Education	Bachelor's degree in business or closely related area; master's degree preferred

Knowledge	Relation of company to the community; diverse rather than specialized knowledge of company operations; familiarity with organizations and people in the community; corporate legal obligations
Skills and abilities	Ability to build rapport with diverse groups and to field difficult questions on the spot; intelligence and wide knowledge; highly polished communications skills

Use Valid Selection Aids

Many companies hire people on the basis of an interview and a review of background. While those are indispensable parts of the selection process, you should use other techniques, too, including assessment centers, job performance tests, or aptitude tests.

These techniques must be job-related and can help you make better hiring decisions. This is because tests and assessment centers are very accurate measurement devices and make it easy to compare all job candidates according to the same scale. They can give you information on technical skills you might not get in an interview or reference check. An expert in testing can develop and validate appropriate selection devices for whatever vacancy you have.

As for the interview itself, ensure that you get all the information you need about the applicant's qualifications. Then ask a number of open-ended questions to find out how much the person knows about the content area. Say, for example, "Tell me what you know about short interval scheduling."

For other skills and abilities, you may need to set up a role-playing situation. For example, let's say you want to find out about the applicant's ability to handle conflict. A direct question will not provide the information you want. But you might describe an imaginary situation and ask the applicant how he or she would respond to it. You might say, for example, "Let's say you have just completed a new marketing program for the company, in your job as marketing director. You present the program to a group of executives. After the presentation an executive says he doesn't like your program one bit. Furthermore, he doesn't care for you as a person and can't understand why the company hired you. How would you handle this?"

Answers to questions like this may give you good insight into more subtle skills and abilities, and they can help you evaluate management style, work habits, creativity, and work-related personal traits. Develop such questions in advance of the interview.

Be Objective

Regardless of the selection techniques you use, be objective in your information gathering. Gather the same kinds of information on all candidates and evaluate it in the same way for each one. That will ensure a fair, objective selection system and will help you identify the best person. Beware of preconceived opinions based on the school the candidate attended, the candidate's former place of employment, or the fact that the candidate is related to one of the managers at your company. That sort of information can lead to the wrong conclusions. Focus instead on the individual applicants and what each has to offer. Look at each with an open mind and draw your own objective conclusions.

Verify Information

In making staffing decisions, it is important to verify all information. If someone claims to have worked at a certain company for ten years, check it out. If another lists an M.B.A. from Harvard, verify it. Do not assume the information is accurate just because it appears on a resume. People do falsify their backgrounds. Similarly, verify the information from an interview by having others interview the person and probe the same areas as you did. In this way you can be assured that your impressions are correct and that you are making the right decisions.

Compile the Information Accurately

Once you have gathered all the necessary information on the job candidates, compile it in some objective way to make the best decision. Some individuals will gather a great deal of information, but then rely on a gut feeling to make a final decision. By doing so, they let much good information go to waste. It is better to fold together the information in a quantitative or qualitative way. Come up with a scoring system or some other means of compiling the information. Think about the strengths and weaknesses of each candidate in comparison with the others.

Look for Creative People
When you select new employees for jobs in your unit, take their creativity into consideration. Look for experience, education, skills, abilities, and personal style, of course, but also probe for creativity. You need employees who can anticipate future problems, who can improve, adapt to changes, and, most important, come up with new solutions.

When you interview job applicants, don't limit yourself to asking, "Have you processed forms before?" Go another step forward: "Have you ever designed new forms without being asked?" or "What ideas do you have for changing forms?" Your means of selecting and promoting people should also include a measurement of creativity.

Closely related to the importance of choosing a good staff is the need to develop your employees to the best of their abilities. One top priority for any manager, as we said earlier, is to develop a potential successor. That could very well speed your own promotion. Take advantage of the most appropriate development aids for your employees. Use college courses, reading materials, professional associations, tutoring, job rotation, and special projects. You will benefit by constantly encouraging your staff to learn and to aspire to greater accomplishments.

Above all, never underestimate the importance of having a good team behind you. You cannot succeed all by yourself. How well you manage human resources will, to a great extent, determine the degree to which you succeed. So select people with the utmost care and make every effort to have extremely well qualified people working for you.

11•

Success at Last

HAVE YOU MADE IT?

> When we are young —and some of us never get over
> it —we are apt to think that applause, conspicuousness and fame
> constitute success. But they are only trappings, the trimmings.
> Success itself is the work, the achievement that evokes these
> manifestations. The man or woman who values the applause more
> than the effort necessary to elicit it is not apt to be deafened —at
> least not for any length of time. Concentrate on your work, and the
> applause will take care of itself.
> —B. C. Forbes

> Someone has well said, "Success is a journey, not a
> destination." Happiness is to be found along the way, not at the end
> of the road, for then the journey is over and it is too late.
> —Robert R. Updegraff

Putting all of the book's suggestions into practice will help you
attain the success you aspire to. But after you've reached your
goals, you may be left wondering, "Have I made it? Am I really
a success?" The answers to those questions depend entirely on
how you define success.

If success, to you, means holding a certain job or earning a certain income, then you are a success if you now have these things. Similarly, you are successful if you attain any other goals you have set for yourself. But there are always more and more goals to attain.

The superstars see no limit to the degree of success they can achieve. They continually strive to attain new goals, and their continuous striving is, of course, one reason they achieve so much. The desire to improve has become a deeply ingrained part of their behavior.

Those who have attained great success don't sit around asking, "Am I successful?" Their focus is always on the future. They might have attained many goals in life, but they see their achievements as only the beginning. They enjoy one triumph and then aim for another. They do not say, "Well, now that I'm a success, I can sit back and take it easy for the rest of my life." That attitude is completely foreign to the highly successful. And so it should be to you.

If you attain great success, you will not have to advertise the fact; others around you will notice it. Though you need not erect statues of yourself, you should continue to emphasize your strengths, abilities, and accomplishments to others. Be proud to show them what you can do.

In your drive for success, will you eventually reach a certain level and then go no further? As we said earlier, that happens to most people eventually, and it could happen to you. For example, if your goal is to head up the entire sales force of a large corporation, you may spend a number of years working your way toward that goal. But once you attain that top spot you can go no further in a sales capacity in that company. At that point you must decide if you're happy in that spot or if you need to go higher.

A highly successful person would at that point begin to work toward the next goal. Perhaps the new goal is to be executive vice-president of sales, marketing, and customer service. The highly successful may start to work on this new goal before attaining the former goal. That is how strong their confidence is. So there is never a point where you can go no further with success. You may have to add or modify goals, but you can always continue to go higher and higher.

Some people equate success with material objects such as mansions, diamonds, and yachts. Certainly material objects can provide a yardstick as to how much success you have attained, but that is only one way of measuring success. You can use many other yardsticks. Think, for example, of status, awards, peer recognition, media attention, and the personal sense of attaining tough goals. Those rewards may not result in direct material benefit, but they are nonetheless signs of success. But success, as we said, means different things to different people. If you want to measure it strictly by material objects, that is your choice.

To gain that success, always focus your efforts on being one of the best in your field of endeavor. If you continually make progress toward that goal, and if you eventually become one of the best, then you will almost certainly attain material rewards. The best business people, attorneys, physicians, artists, musicians, and mechanics are materially successful as well as professionally successful. You need worry only about being the best in your area; the rest will come along with it.

Will attaining great success make you happy? Studies have shown that highly successful people are more satisfied with their lives and their work than those who are less successful. And why shouldn't they be happier? They have attained positions they wanted, accomplished tough goals, earned a great deal, and made influential and important friends. That results in overall satisfaction with their job and life.

Much satisfaction results from the process of attaining success. Happiness is not attained by setting a goal to be happy. Instead, it results indirectly from having accomplished certain highly valued goals. The highly successful have discovered this. They direct their efforts toward accomplishing important goals, and satisfaction comes along as an indirect benefit. So strive to attain goals that are important to you, and you will find yourself happy as a consequence.

HELPING HANDS

When you see a turtle on top of a fence post, you
know he didn't get there by himself.
—Robert J. Lamont

Lefty Gomez was asked the secret of his remarkable World
Series pitching record. "Clean living and a fast outfield" was his reply.

This book has placed a heavy emphasis on things *you* can do to attain success. And that is exactly as it should be, for success will result largely from your own individual efforts. If you understand yourself, develop the right skills and knowledge, are highly motivated, persevere, and become an effective leader, then you are likely to be a success. But as we said in Chapter 10, success in any endeavor is enhanced by others. Assistance might come from your staff, superiors, co-workers, or friends. These people will provide the helping hands you need to enable you to attain what you want. Others can help by teaching you skills, giving you information, providing resources, and doing work for you.

In your quest for success, you must understand how others can assist you, and you must learn to take advantage of their help whenever you need it. Be aware of and receptive to the various kinds of assistance that are available to you.

Mentors
Throughout your professional career it is extremely beneficial to have a mentor, someone who can ease you into the job and train you in the technical aspects of it. This mentor is someone who can show you the ropes and help you build up your knowledge, skills, and abilities. Some companies provide new employees with a mentor who keeps in touch during the new person's first year or two. Most senior employees are flattered to be chosen as a mentor, and new employees appreciate their assistance.

If you do not have an official mentor, seek one out on your own. Select someone who is particularly competent and ask him or her for advice and counsel. Do not say, "Will you be my mentor?" That's not the way it's done. The mentor could be your boss, a superior in another area, a peer, or even someone outside your company.

The help of a mentor is particularly critical at the early stages of your career when you are still building up your basic skills and knowledge. You will also find your mentor helpful when you move to a new functional area or when you're promoted to a higher-level job. The mentor may see you as a protégé and potential successor because of your keen interest in his or her area of responsibility. That could help you receive a future promotion.

Role Models

As we mentioned much earlier, one effective means of getting ahead is to model yourself after someone who is already working at a higher level. The role model you select should be highly successful and respected. Once you've chosen a highly successful person, observe that person's behavior, style, skills, and techniques, and pattern yourself after him or her. If you admire several top-level people, combine the best qualities of each person into a composite role model. Your goal is to become as similar as possible to those who currently hold the jobs you aspire to. When such positions become vacant, you will be seen as a possible successor because you are so much like the incumbents.

Performance Feedback

It is hard to look at oneself objectively. For one reason or another, you may not recognize your own weaknesses, and that hampers your growth and development. In this area, you can seek the assistance of your boss or another trusted person who can give you performance feedback. Ask this person to tell you what areas of your performance need improvement. Seek out someone who will tell you in a straightforward manner what you're doing wrong. Be open to constructive criticism and show your willingness to improve.

Financial Assistance

Whatever the nature of your enterprise, at some point you may require financial assistance from others. Unless you are unusually wealthy, you may have to depend on others to provide working capital. To obtain this financial assistance, put together an objective, succinct proposal and present it to the person who will make the decision to lend or not lend money to you.

Technical Assistance

You may also depend on others for various kinds of technical assistance, such as information on products or services, marketing strategies, or cash flow management. You may get this kind of assistance by hiring consultants to give you advice, or you may ask for help from an employee who has the know-how you need. The expertise of others can be of great value to you.

Staff and Peers

One last form of assistance you need comes from your peers and from those who report to you. Your staff, of course, is there to help you accomplish your goals. You know they're good, because you're the one who hired them, so don't hesitate to ask for their help in making a decision about how to get things done faster or better.

Your peers can give you advice, especially if you need information about the operations or people in their particular work units. Seek out the assistance of peers wherever this can be helpful.

The degree of success you attain will depend for the most part on your own efforts, but you must never hesitate to ask for help when you need it.

SUCCESS FULFILLED

You see things and you say, "Why?" But I dream
things that never were and I say, "Why not?"
—George Bernard Shaw

The life of every man is a diary in which he means to
write one story and writes another; and his humblest hour is when he
compares the volume as it is with what he vowed to make.
—J. M. Barrie

Success will result from your actual accomplishments, not from your dreams or hopes. Those dreams show you where you want to go, but you need to translate the dreams into action. Success results from doing, not merely thinking about doing. Success will not come to you automatically; you must pursue it vigorously in a chase that never ends.

To evaluate where you are right now in your quest for success, reflect on your achievements up to now. On a sheet of paper list all of your significant successes and achievements to date. Ask yourself what people would remember about you if you vanished tomorrow. What products, services, or ideas would you leave behind?

If your list of accomplishments is short or weak, set out today to change things. Your accomplishments need not appear in an encyclopedia or become common knowledge. A great deal of success can be achieved in quieter ways. However, you should be able to take pride in some worthwhile accomplishments in your chosen field, so start now to put together a plan for achieving greater success.

To attain great success you will need courage. The higher you aim the greater the risks will be, and the possibility of failure will loom large. But if you are willing to take those risks, then forge ahead, for the rewards are tremendous when you fully realize your potential.

The safe, secure route may fulfill your basic needs, but you may never become extremely successful that way. The riskier, less conventional path is often the one that leads to spectacular accomplishments. Consider two examples.

The nineteenth-century British scientist John Dalton was a meticulous man of very regular habits. In his research he maintained very detailed records and measurements. For over fifty-seven years he measured the daily rainfall, temperature, and other meteorological data for the city where he resided. He recorded these measurements in ledgers, which grew into many volumes over the years. From all of this detailed, meticulous, conventional, and probably boring work came absolutely nothing. Dalton never became famous for his work as a meteorologist. No one ever quoted him or used his data.

But Dalton had an unanswered question in his mind about the weights of molecules. This took him into uncharted territory, for not much was known about molecular weights at that time. It was a risky field of endeavor, for he had no way of knowing what, if anything, he could accomplish. But Dalton's experiments produced results that eventually led to modern atomic theory. Dalton, between 1803 and 1808, determined the relative weights of atoms and discovered the process by which atoms combine to form molecules, and thereby won a place in the history annals. He would never have accomplished this if he had not been willing to pursue a risky enterprise.

Another man who struck out into uncharted territory was Sir Isaac Newton, who is regarded by many as perhaps the greatest scientist who ever lived. While still in his early twenties, Newton developed the form of mathematics known as calculus. Because of this and other accomplishments, he became chairman of the mathematics department at Cambridge University at the age of twenty-six. Newton is perhaps most famous for his development of the laws of universal gravitation. Those laws enabled us to understand the gravitational forces between the planets and all other objects in the universe. Newton mapped out many other laws that led to the development of modern-day physics, and it was he who discovered that sunlight could be broken into different colored wavelengths of light. He pioneered many of the early advances dealing with light and optics that contributed to our present knowledge about these areas.

As a result of his remarkable accomplishments, Newton was the most prominent scientist in Europe from the 1660s till his death in 1727. Yet, for some unknown reason, this man who asked very complex, unconventional questions accepted a conventional position as Master of the Mint in London in 1696. He remained there until his retirement. From Newton's work at the mint came absolutely nothing. He is not remembered for his work there, and he did nothing of note. This very unconventional man is remembered for his great scientific accomplishments, not his work at the mint.

Both Dalton and Newton attained great success by taking risks and pursuing fields that ideally matched their interests and abilities. From their more conventional, safe pursuits came nothing worth remembering. This is not to say that being the director of a mint or a meteorologist is a waste of time in the pursuit of success. It is to say that Dalton and Newton were talented scientists who were not ideally suited to these other pursuits. Someone else might choose a career as a physicist when he or she could attain much greater success as the director of a mint.

The point is that switching to the career area which is ideal for you takes courage and has risks associated with it, particularly if you must make a switch later in life. But to attain maximum success, you must be willing to take such a step. There is no telling what you might accomplish in your ideal area. The payoff is extremely great for pursuing the less trodden path, but you must have the courage to do so.

This book has provided you with the ideas on how to become a success. Your next step is to put this material into practice. Success is not an elusive phenomenon, nor is it the result of chance. You can understand and manage it just as you would manage other facets of your life. You can attain success if you implement all of the suggestions. The result will be a life rich in accomplishment and satisfaction. And that is something everyone wants and many can attain by taking the proper action. Be one of the highly successful ones.

FINAL THOUGHT

It ain't over till it's over.
—Yogi Berra

Index